Message from Richard Cordray

Director of the CFPB

On July 21, 2011, the Consumer Financial Protection Bureau was launched as the first government agency solely dedicated to consumer financial protection. Debt collection constitutes one of today's most important consumer financial concerns, as indicated by the more than 200,000 consumer complaints that Federal agencies received in 2013 about the conduct of debt collectors. This report describes efforts the Federal government has taken in the past year to administer the Fair Debt Collection Practices Act ("FDCPA"). Among many activities related to debt collection in the past year, three are particularly noteworthy.

First, in July 2013, the Bureau began accepting debt collection complaints. Since it began accepting debt collection complaints through the end of the calendar year, the CFPB has handled approximately 30,300 of these complaints. Debt collection is now our largest source of complaints per month. The Bureau forwards such complaints to debt collectors for review and response, which assists consumers in resolving their complaints.

Second, in November 2013, the Bureau issued an Advanced Notice of Proposed Rulemaking ("ANPR") on the topic of debt collection. The Bureau is the first Federal agency with the authority to issue comprehensive rules for debt collectors. The ANPR reflects prior Federal agency work on debt collection, including a joint FTC-CFPB Roundtable in June 2013 addressing data integrity and information flows. The ANPR is a preliminary step in a process to potentially develop rules to enhance protection for consumers without imposing unnecessary burden or undue costs on collectors. Through its ANPR, the Bureau is collecting information on a wide array of issues, including the accuracy of information used by debt collectors, consumers' knowledge of their rights, and the communication methods collectors employ to recover debts.

The comment period for the ANPR recently closed, and we received more than 20,000 responses that will assist us in potentially developing rules for debt collectors.

Third, through its extensive and continuing supervision and enforcement activities, the Bureau has demonstrated its commitment to prevent and deter collectors from violating the law. In its enforcement work, the Bureau continues to collaborate closely with the Federal Trade Commission, including jointly filing amicus briefs on important issues of law.

Above all, we are concerned about the system-wide problems in the debt collection market that pose risks to consumers, and we want to see good practices come to dominate the market. The Bureau recognizes that these goals are best met when consumers are treated with dignity and respect, and businesses are able to operate fairly and reasonably to collect the debts they are legitimately owed. We will work closely with all stakeholders to achieve a better marketplace. Both consumers and responsible businesses stand to benefit from the creation and application of better and clearer debt collection standards.

Sincerely,

Richard Cordray

Table of contents

1. Introduction

The Consumer Financial Protection Bureau ("CFPB" or "the Bureau") is pleased to submit to Congress its third annual report summarizing its activities to administer the Fair Debt Collection Practices Act ("FDCPA"), 15 U.S.C. § 1692 *et seq*.

The Bureau shares overall FDCPA enforcement responsibility with the Federal Trade Commission ("FTC" or "Commission"). The FTC has provided the Bureau with a letter summarizing its debt collection activities during the past year. Information about the FTC's activities is incorporated into this report, and the FTC's letter is included as Attachment A. The Bureau is grateful to the FTC for assistance in preparing this report. As detailed in this report, the Bureau and FTC closely collaborate to promote efficient and effective coordination on debt collection matters.[1]

This report (1) provides background on the debt collection market; (2) summarizes the Bureau's consumer response function and the number and types of consumer complaints about debt collection that the Bureau and the FTC received in 2013; (3) describes the Bureau's debt collection supervision program; (4) presents developments in the Bureau's and FTC's law enforcement and advocacy programs; (5) discusses the Bureau's and FTC's education and outreach initiatives; and (6) discusses the Bureau's ANPR, as well as additional Bureau and FTC research and policy initiatives.

---

[1] *See* Memorandum of Understanding Between the Consumer Financial Protection Bureau and the Federal Trade Commission (Jan. 2012), *available at* http://www.ftc.gov/sites/default/files/attachments/press-releases/federal-trade-commission-consumer-financial-protection-bureau-pledge-work-together-protect-consumers/120123ftc-cfpb-mou.pdf. As part of this coordination, CFPB and FTC staff regularly meet to discuss ongoing and upcoming law enforcement, rulemaking, and other activities, share debt collection complaints, cooperate on consumer education efforts in the debt collection arena, and consult on debt collection rulemaking and guidance initiatives.

2. Background

Debt collection is a large, multi-billion dollar industry that directly affects many consumers. In 2013, approximately 30 million individuals, or 14% of American adults, had debt in or subject to the collections process averaging approximately $1,400.[2]

Since the advent of the FDCPA in 1977, the industry has experienced dramatic growth along with significant evolution in business practices. The advent and growth of debt buying is one of the most significant changes to the debt collection market. Debt buyers purchase defaulted debt from original creditors or other owners of debt and thereby acquire ownership of the debt. They seek to collect on purchased debts themselves, place the debts with third-party collectors, or resell the debts to other debt buyers. Credit card debt comprises a large majority of the debt that debt buyers purchase.[3] Although over 500 debt buyers are currently active, the market is fairly concentrated, with about 10 firms purchasing a large proportion of the debt that is sold.[4]

Another recent change in the industry is the growth of medical debt in collection. More consumers are affected by medical debt than any other type of debt other than mortgages and

---

[2] Fed. Reserve Bank of N.Y., *Quarterly Report on Household Debt and Credit* (Nov. 2013), *available at* http://www.newyorkfed.org/householdcredit/2013-Q3/HHDC_2013Q3.pdf.

[3] U.S. Gov't Accountability Office, GAO-09-748, *Fair Debt Collection Practices Act Could Better Reflect the Evolving Debt Collection Marketplace and Use of Technology* (2009), *available at* http://www.gao.gov/new.items/d09748.pdf; *see also* U.S. Fed. Trade Comm'n, *The Structure and Practices of the Debt Buying Industry* (2013), *available at* http://www.ftc.gov/os/2013/01/debtbuyingreport.pdf (FTC 2013 Debt Buyer Report).

[4] Robert Hunt, Fed. Reserve Bank of Pa., *Understanding the Model: The Life Cycle of a Debt* (2013), *available at* http://www.ftc.gov/sites/default/files/documents/public_events/life-debt-data-integrity-debt-collection/understandingthemodel.pdf (presented at the FTC-CFPB Roundtable, information about the Roundtable *available at* http://www.ftc.gov/news-events/events-calendar/2013/06/life-debt-data-integrity-debt-collection); *see also* FTC 2013 Debt Buyer Report.

auto loans.[5] Moreover, hospitals and other medical and healthcare providers are now the largest group of customers of collection agencies.

In addition to medical debt, student loan debt in collections is increasing. Over the past decade, student debt has grown by over 33% to average greater than $29,000 for borrowers who graduated in the class of 2012.[6] A growing number of borrowers, greater than one in eight, have student loan debts of $50,000 or more.[7] Student loan debt also comprises a significant portion of third-party debt collection.[8]

In addition to these changes related to the sales and types of debts, perhaps the greatest transformation – and one that is ongoing since the enactment of the FDCPA – relates to the technologies that debt collectors and debt owners[9] use to communicate with consumers. The FDCPA contemplates communications via telephone, postal mail, and telegraph, but it does not reflect the advent of the internet, smartphones, autodialers, fax machines, and social media.[10] These technologies create new opportunities for consumers, debt collectors, and debt owners to communicate in ways that may benefit consumers and be less costly for debt collectors. However, challenges often arise when attempting to apply the FDCPA's prohibitions to technologies that did not exist or were nascent at the time of its enactment.

---

[5] Robert Hunt, Fed. Reserve Bank of Pa., *Understanding the Model: The Life Cycle of a Debt* (2013), *available at* http://www.ftc.gov/sites/default/files/documents/public_events/life-debt-data-integrity-debt-collection/understandingthemodel.pdf (presented at the FTC-CFPB Roundtable).

[6] National Center for Education Statistics, U.S. Dep't of Educ., *2011-2012 National Postsecondary Student Aid Study* (NPSAS:*12*), *available at* http://nces.ed.gov (accessed on March 7, 2014).

[7] Fed. Reserve Bank of N. Y., *Household Debt and Credit: Student Debt*, Slide 6, *available at* http://www.newyorkfed.org/newsevents/mediaadvisory/2013/Lee022813.pdf.

[8] Robert Hunt, Fed. Reserve Bank of Pa., *Understanding the Model: The Life Cycle of a Debt* (2013), *available at* http://www.ftc.gov/sites/default/files/documents/public_events/life-debt-data-integrity-debt-collection/understandingthemodel.pdf (presented at the FTC-CFPB Roundtable).

[9] For purposes on this report, the term "debt owner" includes both creditors and debt buyers.

[10] In 2009, the FTC published a report that focused in part on the issues raised by changes in debt collection technologies. *See 2009 FTC Modernization Report*; FTC Workshop: *Debt Collection 2.0- Protecting Consumers as Technologies Change* (April 28, 2011). Additional information about the Workshop is available at http://www.ftc.gov/bcp/workshops/debtcollectiontech.

Although the market has changed, the debt collection industry remains a top source of consumer complaints for the FTC. In addition, although the Bureau began accepting complaints only a relatively short time ago, debt collection is now its largest source of consumer complaints per month. Not only do these unlawful debt collection practices harm consumers, but debt collectors who refrain from using such practices should not be competitively disadvantaged. As described in detail below, the Bureau and the FTC are using a wide variety of tools to protect consumers from debt collectors who violate the FDCPA or who otherwise engage in deceptive, unfair, abusive, or unlawful collection practices.

3. Consumer complaints

Many consumers submit complaints about debt collectors to Federal agencies. In July 2013, the CFPB began accepting and compiling consumer complaints about debt collection in its Consumer Response system. The Bureau forwards these complaints to companies for review and response. Data from these complaints is sent to the FTC. Using the Bureau's information, as well as complaints submitted directly to it by consumers and from other Federal and State agencies, the FTC compiles consumer complaints in its Consumer Sentinel system and makes them available to Federal and State law enforcement.

As described below, the Bureau and the FTC collect and analyze complaints in different ways to fulfill the unique responsibilities of each agency. The CFPB's complaint handling process focuses on collecting, investigating, and responding to the complaints.[11] The Bureau also uses these complaints for law enforcement purposes. The FTC uses consumer complaints generally to monitor the industry, select targets for investigation, and conduct preliminary analysis that, with further factual development, might reveal or help prove a law violation.

Taken together, the 2013 consumer complaint data collected by both agencies reveal reports of important common consumer harms. Large numbers of consumers, for example, submitted complaints to both agencies that related to inappropriate collections activity, including alleged harassment or misrepresentations by debt collectors. The emergence of these trends helps direct the Bureau and the FTC in their respective consumer protection functions.

---

[11] *See* Dodd-Frank Wall Street Reform and Consumer Protection Act, Pub. L. No. 111-203, § 1021(c)(2), 124 Stat. 1376, 1979 (2010). ("Dodd-Frank Act").

3.1 Consumer complaints submitted to the CFPB

Collecting, investigating, and responding to consumer complaints are integral parts of the CFPB's work.[12] The CFPB's Office of Consumer Response ("Consumer Response") began operations on July 21, 2011 with its acceptance of consumer complaints about credit cards. The Bureau now also accepts complaints about debt collection, mortgages, bank accounts and services, private student loans, vehicle and other consumer loans, credit reporting, money transfers, and payday loans. The Bureau continues to work toward expanding its complaint-handling capacity to include other products and services, such as prepaid cards. Consumers may also contact the CFPB with questions about other products and services.

The Bureau answers questions and refers consumers to other regulators or additional resources as appropriate. The CFPB accepts consumer complaints through its website and by telephone, mail, email, fax, and referral. Consumers submit complaints on the Bureau's website using complaint forms tailored to specific products and can follow up by using a secure consumer portal to check the status of the complaint and review a company's response. While on the website, consumers can chat with a live agent to receive help completing a complaint form. Consumers can also call the Bureau's toll-free number to, among other things, ask questions, submit a complaint, and check the status of a complaint.[13]

Number and Types of Complaints Received

Since it began accepting debt collection complaints on July 10, 2013 through the end of the 2013 calendar year, the CFPB handled approximately 30,300 debt collection complaints. These

---

[12] *See* Dodd-Frank Act, Pub. L. No. 111-203, § 1021(c)(2) (2010).

[13] The CFPB's U.S.-based contact centers handle calls with little-to-no wait times. The contact centers provide services to consumers in more than 180 languages, and to hearing- and speech-impaired consumers via a toll-free telephone number. Cutting-edge technology, including secure company and consumer portals, makes the process safe, efficient, and user-friendly for consumers and companies.

complaints include first-party (owners collecting on their own debts) and third-party collections. Table 1 shows the types of debt collection complaints the CFPB has received.[14]

TABLE 1:   TYPES OF CONSUMER COMPLAINTS

Types of debt collection complaints	%
Continued attempts to collect debt not owed	34%
Communication tactics	23%
Taking/threatening an illegal action	14%
Disclosure about and verification of debt	13%
False statements or representation	9%
Improper contact or sharing of information	8%
Total debt collection complaints	**100%**[15]

For each type of complaint listed in Table 1, consumers also select additional subtopics when submitting the complaint. These subtopics provide more details about the complaint. The following paragraphs describe the subtopics raised by consumers within each topic:

As indicated in the Table at line 1, the most common type of debt collection complaint is about continued attempts to collect a debt that the consumer reports is not owed. The vast majority of consumers submitting complaints about continued attempts to collect a debt report that the debt is not their debt (65%) or that the debt was paid (27%), while the remaining percentage of consumers report that the debt resulted from identity theft (5%) or the debt was discharged in bankruptcy (4%). In many of these cases, the attempt to collect the debt is not itself the

---

[14] The Bureau recognizes that, for a variety of reasons, the debt collection complaints it receives may understate or overstate the extent of debt collector law violations. The FTC recognizes the same limitation with regard to the debt collection complaints it receives. *See* discussion in Section 3.2.

[15] Percentages do not equal 100 percent due to rounding.

problem; rather, consumers assert that the calculation of the amount of underlying debt is inaccurate or unfair. In other cases, the consumer complains about the furnishing of information to credit reporting agencies. These complaints, which are often consistent with complaints consumers submit to the Bureau about credit reporting, suggest that consumers frequently only learn about debt collection accounts when they check their credit reports.

As indicated at line 2 of Table 1, complaints about the communication tactics that are used when collecting debts are also common. Many of these types of complaints are about improper telephone calls. The majority of complaints about communication tactics are about frequent or repeated calls (55%). Often, these complaints stem from being called about another person's debt. Sometimes the call is for someone with a similar name. More often, it appears the consumer's phone number has mistakenly been included in the collector's information about another person's account. Consumers often complain to the CFPB when the collector continues to call even after the consumer has repeatedly told the collector that the alleged debtor cannot be contacted at the dialed number. They also complain about debt collectors calling their places of employment or third parties. Other communication tactics complaints relate to reports of companies threatening to take legal action (30%), using obscene, profane, or abusive language (2%), calling after being sent written cease of communication notice (1%), or calling outside of 8 a.m. to 9 p.m. (1%). Another common type of complaint involves consumers' disputes about debts. The FDCPA requires collectors to provide consumers with validation notices to inform them, among other things, of their rights to dispute debts, but some consumers complain that debt collectors do not provide a validation notice in connection with the collectors' initial communication to collect (23%). Even more consumers raise the concern that when they exercise their rights to dispute debts, collectors do not provide them with documentation that consumers believe they need to verify the debt (e.g., documents showing they signed the underlying credit contract) (70%) (see line 4 of Table 1). The complaints related to disputed debts also reveal confusion on the part of consumers as to when and how they can dispute a debt.[16] Other consumers report that the company did not disclose that the communication was an attempt to collect a debt (7%).

---

[16] As discussed in Section 6.1, the Bureau has developed and made available a form letter to assist consumers in disputing debts.

Consumers also commonly report that the company is taking or threatening to take an illegal action (see line 3 of Table 1). Most of these complaints are about threats to arrest or jail consumers if they do not pay (60%). Other complaints relate to lawsuits including threats to sue on a debt that is too old (17%), being sued without proper notification of the lawsuit (7%), or being sued in a place that is different from where the consumer lives or where the consumer signed the contract (2%). Consumers also complain about seizures or attempts to seize property (6%) or collection or attempts to collect exempt funds such as child support or unemployment benefits (5%).

The majority of complaints about false statements or representations (see line 5 of Table 1) are about attempts to collect the wrong amount from the consumer (50%). Consumers also commonly report that companies impersonated an attorney or a law enforcement or government official (31%), indicated the consumer committed a crime by not paying debt (16%), or indicated that the consumer should not respond to a lawsuit (2%).

For consumers submitting complaints about improper contact or sharing of information (line 6 of Table 1), consumers most often report the company talked to a third party about the debt (47%), contacted an employer after being asked not to do so (27%), or contacted the consumer after being asked not to do so (24%). A less common complaint relates to consumers reporting that they are contacted directly, instead of the debt collector contacting their attorney (2%).

Responses to Complaints Received

The CFPB has sent approximately 11,000 (36%) of the about 30,300 debt collection complaints it has received to companies for their review and response. The CFPB has referred some of the remaining debt collection complaints to other regulatory agencies (35%), while other complaints were found to be incomplete (13%), or are pending with the consumer or the CFPB (16%).

Companies have already responded to approximately 9,000 complaints or 82% of the about 11,000 complaints sent to them for response. Consumers have disputed approximately 1,500 company responses (17%) to their complaints.

The following table shows how companies have responded to consumer complaints.

TABLE 2:   HOW COMPANIES HAVE RESPONDED TO CONSUMER COMPLAINTS TO THE CFPB

How companies have responded to consumer complaints:		%
Company reported closed with monetary relief	200	2%
Company reported closed with nonmonetary relief	1,900	17%
Company reported closed with explanation	6,500	59%
Company reported closed without relief or explanation	300	3%
Company reported administrative response	300	3%
Company reported that it is reviewing the complaint[17]	1,800	16%
Total company responses	**11,000**	**100%**

---

[17] After a complaint is sent to the company for response, the company reviews the information, communicates with the consumer as needed, and determines what action to take in response. The CFPB requests that companies respond to complaints within 15 calendar days. If a complaint cannot be closed within 15 calendar days, a company may indicate that its work on the complaint is "In progress" and provide a final response within 60 calendar days. The complaints awaiting a final company response are reflected by the "Company reviewing" category.

3.2 Consumer complaints submitted to the FTC

The FTC receives information about the conduct of debt collectors from complaints consumers file with the FTC and from its enforcement work.[18] Based on the FTC's experience, it believes many consumers never file complaints with anyone other than the debt collector itself. Other consumers complain only to the underlying creditor or to enforcement agencies other than the FTC. Some consumers may not be aware that the conduct they have experienced violates the FDCPA or that the FTC enforces the FDCPA. For these reasons, the total number of consumer complaints the FTC receives may understate the extent to which the practices of debt collectors violate the law.

On the other hand, the FTC acknowledges that not all of the debt collection practices about which consumers complain necessarily comprise legal violations. Many consumers complain of conduct that, if accurately described, would indeed violate the FDCPA, or Section 5 of the Federal Trade Commission Act ("FTC Act"), 15 U.S.C. § 45. The FTC, however, does not verify whether the information consumers provide is accurate unless the agency undertakes such an inquiry in connection with its law enforcement activities. Moreover, even if accurately described, some conduct about which consumers complain does not violate the FDCPA. Finally, in some cases, consumers may complain of conduct about which more information is needed to determine if the conduct violated the law.

Despite these limitations, the FTC continues to believe that consumer complaint data provides useful insight into the acts and practices of debt collectors. Appendices B and C of the FTC's letter describe trends in the debt collection complaints reported directly to the agency in each of the past two years.[19] To convey the relative impact of a particular practice on consumers during

---

[18] Consumers may file complaints with the FTC via its toll-free hotline (1-877-FTC-HELP), online complaint forms at https://www.ftccomplaintassistant.gov/or United States mail.

[19] The figures in these appendices relate to complaints filed directly with the FTC. In contrast, complaint figures in the Federal Trade Commission's annual Consumer Sentinel Network Data Book include both complaints submitted to the FTC and those complaints originally submitted to certain other entities that partner with the FTC through its Consumer Sentinel network. *See* FTC, CONSUMER SENTINEL NETWORK DATA BOOK FOR JANUARY-DECEMBER 2013 at 2-3 and 6 (Feb. 2014), *available at* http://www.ftc.gov/reports/consumer-sentinel-network-data-book-january-december-2013. For this reason, the total number of debt collection complaints set forth in this report as "FTC complaints" is fewer than the number stated in the FTC's annual Consumer Sentinel Network Data Book.

the past year, the appendices to the FTC's letter include the percentage of all 2013 FTC complaints related to each specific practice. In addition, to assist in identifying trends over time, the appendices compare the percentage of all FDCPA complaints to the FTC in 2012 and 2013 regarding a certain practice.

3.2.1 Total number of FTC complaints

Hundreds of thousands of consumers contact the FTC every year about consumer protection issues. With respect to debt collection, the FTC receives both consumer inquiries and complaints. In general, consumer complaints concern the alleged behavior of specific actors, whereas consumer inquiries ask for information about legal rights or other topics. The FTC's Consumer Response Center ("CRC") makes every effort to distinguish between these two categories of contacts. The data presented in the appendices include only consumer contacts that the CRC has identified as complaints.

ALL COLLECTORS

The FTC continues to receive more complaints about the debt collection industry than any other specific industry. In 2013, the total number of debt collection complaints the FTC received from all sources rose to 204,464, up from 202,616 in 2012.[20] Of that total, approximately 73,211 complaints were filed directly with the FTC—a figure that accounts for 17% of all complaints filed directly with the agency. These complaints fall into two industry categories: 60,485 complaints related to third-party debt collectors,[21] and the remaining 12,726 related to in-house debt collectors.[22] This compares with the total of 125,136 direct-to-

---

[20] *See* FTC, CONSUMER SENTINEL NETWORK DATA BOOK FOR JANUARY-DECEMBER 2013 at App. B2 (Feb. 2014), *available at* http://www.ftc.gov/reports/consumer-sentinel-network-data-book-january-december-2013. Note that the 2012 complaint numbers identified in this year's report differ slightly from those identified in last year's report because, in connection with a quality assurance review, the FTC staff reviewed and re-coded some complaints after the 2013 Annual Report was issued.

[21] "Third-party debt collectors" include contingency fee collectors and attorneys who regularly collect or attempt to collect, directly or indirectly, debts asserted to be owed or due another, as well as debt buyers collecting on debts they purchased in default.

[22] Some complaints are directed toward both third-party debt collectors and in-house creditor collectors. Thus, the total number of complaints against all debt collectors is slightly less than the sum of all third-party complaints and all in-house creditor complaints.

FTC complaints in 2012, which accounted for 24.1% of all complaints filed directly with the FTC. Of this total, 102,783 complaints related to third-party debt collectors, and the remaining 22,353 related to in-house debt collectors.

3.2.2 FTC complaints by category

In addition to evaluating the total number of complaints about debt collectors, it also is instructive to consider the specific types of debt collection practices about which consumers complain.[23] Because consumer complaints frequently address more than one debt collection practice, the complaints may have been assigned more than one code by the FTC's CRC.[24]

Table 3 on the next page reflects the relative prevalence of different complaint categories during 2013. The complaint numbers in this table pertain only to complaints filed directly with the FTC, and the percentages are calculated relative to the total number of these complaints that pertain to third-party debt collectors.

---

[23] Because consumer complaints frequently address more than one debt collection practice, the complaint may have been assigned many more than one code by the FTC's CRC. (Each CRC code assigned to an FDCPA complaint corresponds to a potential law violation.) Thus, if one adds together all the complaints for each of the fifteen debt collection codes each year, the total exceeds the number of FDCPA complaints the FTC actually received in that year.

[24] Each CRC code assigned to an FDCPA complaint corresponds to a potential law violation.

TABLE 3: FTC DEBT COLLECTION COMPLAINTS BY FDCPA COMPLAINT CATEGORY[25]

FDCPA Complaint Category	Total 2013 Complaints	Percentage of 2013 FDCPA Complaints
Repeated Calls	23,582	39.0%
Misrepresent Debt Character, Amount, or Status	23,068	38.1%
Falsely Threatens Illegal or Unintended Act	20,627	34.1%
No Written Notice	17,502	28.9%
Falsely Threatens Arrest, Property Seizure	16,882	27.9%
Fails to Identify as Debt Collector	11,941	19.7%
Repeated Calls to Third Parties	10,026	16.6%
Improperly Calls Debtor at Work	9,761	16.1%
Uses Obscene, Profane or Abusive Language	8,652	14.3%
Reveals Debt to Third Party	8,571	14.2%
Refuses to Verify Debt After Written Request	6,361	10.5%
Collects Unauthorized Fees, Interest, or Expenses	5,605	9.3%
Calls Before 8:00 a.m., after 9:00 p.m., or at Inconvenient Times	4,656	7.7%
Calls Debtor After Getting "Cease Communication" Notice	2,906	4.8%
Uses or Threatens Violence	2,502	4.1%

---

[25] This table is included as Appendix C to the FTC's letter.

HARASSING THE ALLEGED DEBTOR OR OTHERS

This complaint category encompasses four distinct violation codes. Under the FDCPA, debt collectors may not harass any person to try to collect on a debt.[26] In 2013, 39% of FDCPA complaints or 23,582 complaints claimed that collectors harassed the complainants by calling repeatedly or continuously. Also in 2013, 14.3% of FDCPA complaints or 8,652 complaints claimed that a collector had used obscene, profane, or abusive language. Allegations that collectors called before 8:00 a.m., after 9:00 p.m., or at other times that the collectors knew or should have known were inconvenient to the consumer, made up 7.7% of complaints or 4,656 complaints in 2013. Reports that collectors used or threatened to use violence if consumers failed to pay accounted for 4.1% of FDCPA complaints in 2013 or 2,502 complaints.

DEMANDING AN AMOUNT OTHER THAN IS PERMITTED BY LAW OR CONTRACT

This category includes two different FDCPA law violation codes. First, the FDCPA prohibits debt collectors from misrepresenting the character, amount, or legal status of a debt.[27] The types of complaints that fall into this category, for example, are reports that a debt collector is attempting to collect either a debt the consumer does not owe at all or a debt amount exceeding that actually owed. Other complaints in this category relate to collectors seeking to collect on debts that have been discharged in bankruptcy. In 2013, there were 23,068 complaints describing this conduct, representing 38.1% of FDCPA complaints.

Second, the FDCPA prohibits debt collectors from collecting any amount unless it is "expressly authorized by the agreement creating the debt or permitted by law."[28] In 2013, 9.3% of FDCPA complaints or 5,605 complaints asserted that collectors demanded interest, fees, or expenses that were not owed (such as unauthorized collection fees, late fees, and court costs).

---

[26] 15 U.S.C. § 1692d.

[27] 15 U.S.C. §1692e(2).

[28] 15 U.S.C §1692f(1).

FAILING TO SEND REQUIRED WRITTEN NOTICE OF THE DEBT TO CONSUMER

The FDCPA requires that debt collectors send consumers a written notice that includes, among other things, the amount of the debt, the name of the creditor to whom the debt is owed, and a statement that, if within thirty days of receiving the notice the consumer disputes the debt in writing, the collector will obtain verification of the debt.[29] Many consumers who do not receive this notice are unaware of the obligation to dispute the debt in writing in order to obtain verification of the debt. In 2013, 28.9% of FDCPA complaints or 17,502 complaints reported that collectors did not provide the required notice.

THREATENING DIRE CONSEQUENCES IF CONSUMER FAILS TO PAY

The FDCPA bars debt collectors from making false threats as to what might happen if the consumer fails to pay the debt, unless the collector has the legal authority and the intent to take the threatened action.[30] In 2013, 34.1% of FDCPA complaints or 20,627 complaints reported that collectors falsely threatened a lawsuit or some other action that they could not or did not intend to take. In addition, 27.9% of FDCPA complaints or 16,882 complaints reported that collectors falsely threatened arrest or property seizure.

FAILING TO IDENTIFY SELF AS A DEBT COLLECTOR

To avoid creating a false or misleading impression, the FDCPA requires a debt collector to disclose in all communications with a consumer that he or she is a debt collector and, in the first communication with the consumer, that he or she is attempting to collect a debt and that any information obtained will be used for that purpose.[31] Consumers who do not receive such notification may reveal information under false pretenses that will later be used against them to

---

[29] 15 U.S.C. § 1692g(a).

[30] 15 U.S.C. § 1692e(4)-(5).

[31] 15 U.S.C. § 1692e(11). This requirement does not apply if the communication at issue is a formal pleading made in connection with a legal action. *Id.* 15 U.S.C. § 1692d(6) also provides that it is generally an abusive practice to place telephone calls without meaningful disclosure of the caller's identity.

collect the alleged debt. In 2013, 19.7% of all FDCPA complaints or 11,941 complaints alleged the collector failed to provide the required "mini-Miranda" warning.

REVEALING ALLEGED DEBT TO THIRD PARTIES

The FDCPA generally prohibits third-party contacts for any purpose other than obtaining information about the consumer's location.[32] Collectors calling to obtain location information also are prohibited from revealing that a consumer allegedly owes a debt.[33]

Improper third-party contacts may embarrass or intimidate consumers who allegedly owe the debts and be a continuing aggravation to third parties. In some cases, collectors reportedly have made misrepresentations as well as used harassing and abusive tactics in their communications with third parties, or even have attempted to collect from them.

Contacts with consumers' employers and co-workers about consumers' alleged debts also may jeopardize continued employment or prospects for promotion. Relationships between consumers and their families, friends, or neighbors may additionally suffer from improper third-party contacts. This past year, 16.6% of FDCPA complaints or 10,026 complaints claimed that collectors called a third party repeatedly to obtain location information about the consumer. The third parties contacted included employers, relatives, children, neighbors, and friends. Also in 2013, 14.2% of all FDCPA complaints, or 8,571 complaints, reported that debt collectors illegally disclosed a purported debt to a third party.

IMPERMISSIBLE CALLS TO CONSUMER'S PLACE OF EMPLOYMENT

Under the FDCPA, a debt collector may not contact a consumer at work if the collector knows or has reason to know that the consumer's employer prohibits such contacts.[34] By continuing to contact consumers at work under these circumstances, debt collectors may put them in

---

[32] 15 U.S.C. § 1692c(b). Location information includes a consumer's home address and telephone number or place of employment. 15 U.S.C. § 1692a(7).

[33] 15 U.S.C. § 1692b(2).

[34] 15 U.S.C. § 1692c(a)(3).

jeopardy of losing their jobs. In 2013, 16.1% of FDCPA complaints or 9,761 complaints related to calls to consumers at work.

FAILING TO VERIFY DISPUTED DEBTS

The FDCPA also mandates that, if a consumer submits a dispute in writing within 30 days of receiving a validation notice, the collector must cease collection efforts until it has provided written verification of the debt.[35] Many consumers complained that collectors ignored their written disputes, sent no verification, and continued collection efforts. Other consumers reported that some collectors continued to contact them about the debts between the date the consumers submitted their dispute and the date the collectors provided the verification. Last year, 10.5% of all FDCPA complaints or 6,361 complaints, claimed that collectors failed to verify disputed debts.

CONTINUING TO CONTACT CONSUMER AFTER RECEIVING "CEASE COMMUNICATION"

Subject to limited exceptions,[36] the FDCPA requires debt collectors to cease all communications with a consumer about an alleged debt if the consumer communicates in writing that he or she wants all such communications to stop or that he or she refuses to pay the alleged debt.[37] This "cease communication" notice does not prevent collectors or creditors from filing suit against the consumer to collect, but it does prohibit collectors from calling the consumer or sending further notices. In 2013, 4.8% of FDCPA complaints or 2,906 complaints reported that collectors ignored "cease communication" notices and continued collection attempts.

---

[35] 15 U.S.C. § 1692g(b).

[36] 15 U.S.C. § 1692g(c)(1)-(3).

[37] 15 U.S.C. § 1692c(c).

4. Bureau supervision of debt collection activities

Under the Dodd-Frank Act, the CFPB has the authority to supervise certain nonbank entities that offer or provide consumer financial products or services.[38] In addition, for other nonbank markets for consumer financial products or services, the Bureau has the authority to supervise "larger participants" as the Bureau defines by rule.

The Bureau began a critical new chapter in debt collection supervision on January 2, 2013, when the CFPB's larger participant rule for debt collection became effective. Under this larger participant rule, the Bureau has supervisory authority over any firm with more than $10 million in annual receipts from consumer debt collection activities. This authority extends to about 175 debt collectors, which accounts for more than 60% of the industry's annual receipts in the consumer debt collection market. This new Federal authority enables the Bureau both to protect consumers and to promote a level playing field for law abiding debt collectors.

In addition to the expansion of its supervisory authority in the debt collection market, the Bureau also issued two supervisory bulletins to provide guidance and feedback to industry on how to comply with the law or to reduce the risk of consumer harm.

---

[38] Specifically, the Bureau has authority to supervise nonbank entities in the residential mortgage, payday lending, and private education lending markets. The Bureau also has the authority to supervise where it has "reasonable cause to determine, by order, after notice to the covered person and a reasonable opportunity for such covered person to respond … that such covered person is engaging, or has engaged, in conduct that poses risks to consumers with regard to the offering or provision of consumer financial products or service." 12 U.S.C. § 5514(a)(1)(C).

4.1 Supervision of the consumer debt collection market

Once the "larger participants" rule went into effect, the Bureau initiated supervisory examinations of this sector of the debt collection market, often working in collaboration with State regulators. These examinations furthered the Bureau's mission of promoting fair, transparent, and competitive consumer financial markets. The examinations also provided the CFPB with valuable insight into industry practices and procedures that, among other things, is helping the Bureau plan its 2014 examinations.

The Bureau examines consumer debt collectors on a risk basis to ensure compliance with the statutory and regulatory requirements of Federal consumer financial laws. The CFPB uses a data-driven approach to assess risk to consumers, collecting information about both the market and individual institutions. Based on the data currently available, entity size is one of the main risk factors. This is because, as a general matter, larger companies engage in a larger number of transactions and, therefore, have a greater impact on consumers. The Bureau also recognizes that consumer risk may arise based on the nature of the entity's conduct. Patterns of consumer complaints about an entity's conduct, for example, can also be a good indicator of risk. The Bureau revisits its risk assessments as it gathers additional data and information, including through the results of its examinations.

In deference to the importance of confidentiality and consistent with the policies of the prudential regulators, the Bureau treats information obtained from companies through the supervisory process as confidential and privileged.[39]

---

[39] *See* 12 C.F.R. pt. 1070; CFPB Bulletin 12-01 (Jan. 4, 2012), *available at*
http://files.consumerfinance.gov/f/2012/01/GC_bulletin_12-01.pdf; *see also* 12 U.S.C. §§ 1821(t), 1828(x).

4.2 CFPB Bulletins related to debt collection

As discussed above, the Bureau issued two bulletins in 2013 that were focused on debt collection. The first bulletin addresses unfair, deceptive, or abusive acts or practices ("UDAAPs") in the collection of consumer debts.[40] The Dodd-Frank Act prohibits all covered persons and service providers (including first-party and third-party debt collectors) from engaging in UDAAPs in the collection of consumer debts. The bulletin clarifies the contours of this obligation by restating and explicating the statutory definitions of such acts and practices, and by providing a non-exhaustive list of industry acts and practices the Bureau will be watching closely.

The second bulletin on debt collection provides guidance to creditors, debt buyers, and third-party debt collectors about complying with the FDCPA and the Dodd-Frank Act when making representations to consumers about the impact that paying debts in collection may have on credit reports, credit scores, and creditworthiness.[41] Together, the FDCPA and the Dodd-Frank Act prohibit covered persons or service providers, including debt collectors and debt owners, from engaging in deception while collecting or attempting to collect on consumer debts.[42] The Bureau has observed in supervisory examinations that debt collectors and debt owners often make representations to consumers about effects of paying debts on credit reports, credit scores, or creditworthiness. The Bureau is concerned that, in certain situations, these representations may be deceptive under the FDCPA, the Dodd-Frank Act, or both. The bulletin provides examples of such potentially deceptive representations and advises debt collectors and debt owners to ensure that any claims they make with respect to the impact that paying debts may have on credit reports, credit scores, and creditworthiness are not deceptive.

---

[40] The bulletin is available at http://files.consumerfinance.gov/f/201307_cfpb_bulletin_unfair-deceptive-abusive-practices.pdf.

[41] The bulletin is available at http://files.consumerfinance.gov/f/201307_cfpb_bulletin_collections-consumer-credit.pdf.

[42] 15 U.S.C. § 1692e; 12 U.S.C. §§ 5531(a), 5536(a)(1)(B).

5. Enforcement

In addition to the Bureau's debt collection rulewriting, supervisory, and consumer response functions, the Bureau also is a law enforcer.[43] Under the Dodd-Frank Act, the CFPB's authority includes investigating and taking enforcement action against providers of consumer financial goods and services (including first-party and third-party debt collectors) that engage in unfair, deceptive, and abusive acts and practices.[44] The Bureau also has the authority to take enforcement action against those who violate the FDCPA.[45]

The FTC is primarily a law enforcement agency, and law enforcement investigations and litigation are at the heart of the FTC's recent debt collection work. Both the FDCPA and the FTC Act authorize the Commission to investigate and take law enforcement action against debt collectors that violate those statutes.[46]

The Bureau and FTC work to coordinate their enforcement actions and, absent exigent circumstances, inform one another prior to initiating an investigation or bringing an

---

[43] Dodd-Frank Act Title X, Subtitle E.

[44] 12 U.S.C. §§ 5531, 5536.

[45] FDCPA § 814, 15 U.S.C. 1692l.

[46] Under the FDCPA, the Commission's authority includes investigating and taking law enforcement action against debt collectors that engage in unfair, deceptive, abusive, or other practices that violate the statute. FDCPA § 814, 15 U.S.C. § 1692l. Under the FTC Act, the FTC's authority includes investigating and taking law enforcement action against entities that, in connection with collecting on debts, engage in unfair or deceptive acts and practices. FTC Act § 5, 15 U.S.C. § 45. More information about the FTC's choice of forum and available remedies is set forth in Attachment A.

enforcement action. This notice prevents duplicative or conflicting enforcement efforts and undue burdens on industry.[47]

5.1 Bureau law enforcement actions

The Bureau announced two new law enforcement actions in 2013 related to debt collection. In November of 2013, the Bureau entered into a consent decree requiring payday lender, Cash America International, Inc. ("Cash America") to refund up to $14 million to consumers for robo-signing court documents in debt collection lawsuits. The Bureau also alleged that Cash America – one of the largest short-term, small-dollar lenders in the country – violated the Military Lending Act by illegally overcharging servicemembers and their families. Cash America also paid a $5 million fine for these violations and for destroying records in advance of the Bureau's examination.

In its complaint, the Bureau alleged that, for nearly five years, Cash America's debt collection subsidiary in Ohio, Cashland Financial Services, Inc., had engaged in unfair and deceptive acts and practices by preparing, executing, and notarizing documents filed in its Ohio collections litigations that did not comply with State and court-required signature rules. Employees manually stamped attorney signatures on legal pleadings and department manager signatures on balance-due and military-status affidavits without prior review, and legal assistants notarized documents without following proper procedures. The Bureau estimates that about 14,000 consumers paid money as a result of debt collection litigation which may have involved reliance on improper filings.

The Bureau also alleged that Cash America illegally overcharged servicemembers and violated the Military Lending Act, which restricts the rate on certain types of loans given to servicemembers to 36 percent. Cash America extended payday loans exceeding that rate to more than 300 active-duty servicemembers or dependents.

---

[47] *See* Memorandum of Understanding Between the Consumer Financial Protection Bureau and the Federal Trade Commission (Jan. 2012), *available at* http://www.ftc.gov/sites/default/files/attachments/press-releases/federal-trade-commission-consumer-financial-protection-bureau-pledge-work-together-protect-consumers/120123ftc-cfpb-mou.pdf.

The Bureau's action followed its routine examination of Cash America's operations, during which the company, among other things, carelessly destroyed records relevant to the Bureau's onsite compliance examination. Specifically, Cash America's online lending subsidiary, Enova Financial, instructed employees to limit the information they provided to the Bureau about their sales and marketing pitches, deleted recorded phone calls with consumers, and continued to shred documents after the Bureau told them to halt such activities. Further, Cash America withheld an internal audit report related to collection practices.

As a result of the enforcement action, Cash America was ordered to refund consumers up to $14 million and pay a $5 million civil monetary penalty. Cash America was also ordered to develop and implement a comprehensive plan to improve its compliance with consumer financial protection laws, including the Military Lending Act. After the Bureau discovered the robo-signing, Cash America also dismissed pending collections lawsuits, terminated all post-judgment collections activities, cancelled all judgments obtained, and corrected information it furnished to credit bureaus for the nearly 14,000 wrongful cases filed in Ohio.

The Bureau's second debt collection enforcement action announced in 2013 was against California-based CashCall, its subsidiary, WS Funding LLC, and its affiliate, Delbert Services Corporation, a Nevada collection agency, all of which are under the common ownership of J. Paul Reddam. Beginning in late 2009, CashCall and WS Funding entered into an arrangement with Western Sky Financial, a South Dakota-based online lender. The loans ranged from $850 to $10,000, and typically had upfront fees, lengthy repayment terms, and annual interest rates from nearly 90% to 343%. Many consumers signed loan agreements permitting loan payments to be debited directly from their bank accounts, similar to a payday lender. The loans were then acquired by WS Funding and serviced by CashCall. In September 2013, Western Sky stopped making loans and began to shut down its business after several States began investigations and court actions. But CashCall and its collection agency, Delbert, have continued to take monthly installment payments from consumers' bank accounts or have otherwise sought to collect money from borrowers.

The Bureau's complaint alleges that defendants CashCall, WS Funding, Delbert, and Reddam violated the Dodd-Frank Act's prohibitions on unfair, deceptive, and abusive acts and practices. The Bureau's investigation showed that the high-cost loans violated either licensing requirements or interest-rate caps – or both – in at least eight States: Arizona, Arkansas, Colorado, Indiana, Massachusetts, New Hampshire, New York, and North Carolina. Under statutes in at least these eight States, any obligation to pay such loans was rendered void or otherwise nullified in whole or in part by law. Therefore, the defendants allegedly are collecting money that consumers do not owe. This action is still pending.

In addition to the Bureau's public enforcement actions involving debt collection practices, the Bureau is also conducting a number of non-public investigations of companies to determine whether they engaged in collection practices that violate the FDCPA or the Dodd-Frank Act.

5.2 FTC law enforcement actions

In recent years, to improve deterrence, the Commission has focused on bringing a greater number of cases and obtaining stronger monetary and injunctive remedies against debt collectors that violate the law. From January 1 through December 31, 2013, the FTC has brought or resolved nine debt collection cases—the highest number of debt collection cases that it has brought or resolved in any single year. The FTC obtained preliminary or permanent injunctive relief in seven Section 13(b) cases involving debt collection and referred two additional cases to the Department of Justice for civil penalties. In several of its Section 13(b) cases, the Commission obtained preliminary relief that included *ex parte* temporary restraining orders with asset freezes, immediate access to business premises, and appointment of receivers to run the debt collection businesses.

The cases discussed below represent a concerted effort by the FTC to target unlawful debt collection practices including false threats, harassment, or abuse and attempts to collect on "phantom" payday loan debts. [48]

Deceptive, Unfair, and Abusive Collector Conduct

Targeting debt collectors that engage in deceptive, unfair, or abusive conduct continues to be one of the Commission's highest priorities. In particular, the Commission continues to pursue

---

[48] In addition to the cases described below, in September 2013, in response to an invitation from the Seventh Circuit, the Commission filed an amicus brief in *Deborah Jackson v. Payday Financial, LLC* expressing its views on the validity of arbitration clauses used by Payday Financial, which purport to require borrowers to resolve all payday loan-related disputes through arbitration conducted on a reservation of the Cheyenne River Sioux Tribe. More information about this case is available in subpart B of the FTC's Letter.

debt collectors that secure payments from consumers by falsely threatening litigation or otherwise falsely implying that they are involved in law enforcement. In 2013, the Commission filed or resolved seven actions alleging deceptive, unfair, or abusive debt collection conduct.

In *FTC v. Forensic Case Management Services, Inc.*, the FTC secured substantial monetary judgments against a debt collection enterprise and a complete ban on future debt collection activity, along with other injunctive relief.[49] The FTC's complaint alleged that the defendants violated the FTC Act and the FDCPA through such egregious conduct as threats of physical harm, obscene and profane language, revealing consumers' debts to third parties, and falsely threatening consumers with lawsuits, arrest, and wage garnishment. The judgments in the case exceed $35.5 million, and despite partial suspension based on the defendants' inability to pay, the Commission collected more than $1.1 million for consumer redress.

In *United States v. Expert Global Solutions, Inc.*, the Commission secured a $3.2 million civil penalty for unlawful collection practices —the highest penalty the FTC has ever obtained against a third-party debt collector.[50] The FTC's complaint charged that the company, operating under several business names including "NCO," violated the FDCPA and the FTC Act by employing harassing collection calls, disclosing consumers' debts to third parties, and continuing collection efforts without verifying debts even after consumers said they did not owe those debts. The settlement prohibits the company from engaging in this unlawful conduct and further requires that whenever a consumer disputes the validity or the amount of a debt, the company must either terminate collection efforts or suspend collection until it conducts a reasonable investigation and verifies that its information about the debt is accurate and complete.

---

[49] *FTC v. Forensic Case Mgmt. Servs., Inc.*, No. 2:11-cv-07484 (C.D. Cal. Jan. 4, 2013) (Final Judgment and Order for Permanent Injunction and Monetary Relief), see also Press Release, *FTC Settlement Obtains Permanent Ban Against Abusive Debt Collection Operation* (Jan. 17, 2013), *available at* http://www.ftc.gov/opa/2013/01/rumson.shtm.

[50] *United States v. Expert Global Solutions, Inc.*, No. 3:13-cv-2611 (N.D. Tex. July 16, 2013) (Stipulated Order for Permanent Injunction and Monetary Judgment); *see also* Press Release, *World's Largest Debt Collection Operation Settles FTC Charges*, Will Pay $3.2 Million Penalty (July 9, 2013), *available at* http://www.ftc.gov/news-events/press-releases/2013/07/worlds-largest-debt-collection-operation-settles-ftc-charges-will.

In *United States v. National Attorney Collection Services, Inc.*, the Commission brought its first enforcement action involving the use of text messages to collect debts.[51] The Commission's complaint alleged that the company sent consumers English- and Spanish-language text messages that falsely portrayed the company as a law firm and failed to disclose that it was a debt collector. The company also illegally revealed debts to consumers' family members, friends, and co-workers through the use of mailing envelopes that pictured a large arm shaking money from a consumer being held upside down. The settlement imposed a $1 million civil penalty, requires the company to obtain consumers' express consent before contacting them by text message, and bars the company from making deceptive legal threats, falsely holding itself out to be a law firm, revealing debts to third parties, and omitting required disclosures.

The Commission also obtained an *ex parte* temporary restraining order and other extraordinary relief to shut down a debt collection enterprise permeated by unlawful conduct. In *FTC v. Asset & Capital Management Group*, a U.S. District Court entered a temporary restraining order with an asset freeze, receivership, and immediate access to the business premises against a debt collector that the FTC alleged extorted payments from consumers by using false threats of lawsuits and calculated campaigns to embarrass consumers by unlawfully communicating with family members, friends, and coworkers.[52] The FTC's complaint also alleged that the company failed to notify consumers of their right to dispute and obtain verification of their debts, and that its collectors failed to disclose the name of the company they represented, and that they were attempting to collect a debt, during calls to consumers. The Commission continues to litigate the *Asset & Capital Management* matter.

In *FTC v. Security Credit Services, LLC*, the Commission alleged that a debt collection enterprise falsely threatened consumers with lawsuits and misled consumers into paying

---

[51] *Complaint, United States v. Nat'l Attorney Collection Servs., Inc.*, No. 2:13-cv-6212 (C.D. Cal. Aug. 23, 2013); *see also* Press Release, *FTC Brings First Case Alleging Text Messages Were Used In Illegal Debt Collection Scheme* (Sept. 25, 2013), *available at* http://www.ftc.gov/news-events/press-releases/2013/09/ftc-brings-first-case-alleging-text-messages-were-used-illegal.

[52] *FTC v. Asset & Capital Mgmt. Grp., LLC*, No. CV13-5267 (C.D. Cal. July 24, 2013) (ex parte TRO); *see also* Press Release, *At FTC's Request, Court Orders Halt to Debt Collector's Illegal Practices, Freezes Assets* (Aug. 1, 2013), *available at* http://www.ftc.gov/news-events/press-releases/2013/08/ftcs-request-court-orders-halt-debt-collectors-illegal-practices.

unnecessary fees.[53] The FTC's complaint alleged that the company violated the FTC Act and the FDCPA by deceiving consumers into using a payment method that required a substantial "convenience fee." In addition, while one defendant in this case was a law firm that in some instances sued consumers for nonpayment, the complaint alleged that the firm regularly threatened to sue consumers where it did not have the authority to do so or in jurisdictions where it was not licensed to practice law, in violation of the FDCPA. The settlement in this case stops the false threats of suit and secures nearly $800,000 in restitution for consumers for deceptively-obtained convenience fees.

Finally, the FTC recently settled allegations in *FTC v. AMG Services, Inc.* that a payday lender, collecting on its own behalf, violated the FTC Act by falsely threatening to take legal action against consumers.[54] The Commission also obtained a temporary restraining order with an asset freeze in *FTC v. Goldman Schwartz*—a case alleging that the defendant falsely threatened consumers with arrest, disclosed consumers' debts to third parties, collected unauthorized fees, engaged in harassing and abusive conduct, failed to provide required notices, and made collection calls before 8:00 a.m. and after 9:00 p.m.[55]

Phantom debt collection

One of the Commission's major consumer protection concerns is the continuing rise of so-called "phantom debt collectors." Phantom debt collectors engage in unfair, deceptive, or abusive conduct by attempting to collect on debts that either do not exist or are not owed to the phantom

---

[53] *FTC v. Security Credit Services, LLC*, No. 1:13-cv-799 (N.D. Ga. Mar. 19, 2013) (Stipulated Final Judgment and Order for Permanent Injunction); *see also* Press Release, *In Settlement with FTC, Debt Collectors Agree to Stop Deceiving Consumers and Pay Nearly $800,000* (Mar. 26, 2013), *available at* http://www.ftc.gov/news-events/press-releases/2013/03/settlement-ftc-debt-collectors-agree-stop-deceiving-consumers-and.

[54] *FTC v. AMG Services, Inc.*, No. 2:12-cv-536 (D. Nev. July 18, 2013) (Agreed Joint Motion to Enter Stipulated Order for Permanent Injunction and Judgment); *see also* Press Release, *AMG Defendants Settle FTC's Debt Collection Charges* (July 22, 2013), *available at* http://www.ftc.gov/news-events/press-releases/2013/07/amg-defendants-settle-ftc's-debt-collection-charges. The Commission continues to litigate other aspects of its case against AMG Services.

[55] Complaint, *FTC v. Goldman Schwartz*, No. 4:13-cv-106 (S.D. Tex. Jan. 31, 2013); *see also* Press Release, *FTC Action Leads to Shutdown of Texas-based Debt Collector that Allegedly Used Deception, Insults, and False Threats Against Consumers* (Jan. 31, 2013), *available at* http://www.ftc.gov/opa/2013/01/goldman.shtm.

debt collector. In the past year, the Commission has filed or resolved two actions against phantom debt collectors.

In September 2013, in *FTC v. Pro Credit Group, LLC*, a U.S. district court entered a set of stipulated permanent injunctions and judgments totaling $67.5 million against the defendants for violations of the FTC Act and the Commission's Telemarketing Sales Rule, 16 C.F.R. Part 310.[56] The complaint alleged that the defendants, working closely with an overseas call center in India, defrauded consumers out of millions of dollars by collecting payments for debts that the consumers did not owe to them or did not owe at all. The victims of this scam include consumers who previously applied for or received loans from online payday loan companies and supplied sensitive personal financial information in the process—information that eventually made its way to the defendants. The settlements ban defendants from engaging in telemarketing, debt collection, debt relief services, and/or the sale of financial-related goods or services, depending on the individual defendant's role in the enterprise. The settlement also includes an unsuspended judgment of approximately $25 million against one of the individual defendants, and while monetary judgments against the other defendants were largely suspended based on inability to pay, defendants were all required to turn over cash on hand, real estate, and other significant assets.

In *FTC v. Pinnacle Payment Services, LLC*, the Commission charged that defendants, working out of offices in Atlanta and Cleveland, collected and processed millions of dollars in payment for phantom debts using robo-calls and voice messages that threatened legal action and arrest unless consumers responded within a few days.[57] Callers also often claimed an affiliation with a law firm or a law enforcement agency. The Commission obtained an *ex parte* temporary restraining order with an asset freeze, receivership, and immediate access against the defendants, and the court hearing the matter recently entered a preliminary injunction.

---

[56] *FTC v. Pro Credit Grp., LLC*, No. 8:12-cv-586 (M.D. Fla. Sept. 5, 2013) (stipulated final judgments as to all remaining defendants); *see also* Press Release, *FTC Settlement Bans Defendants from Engaging in Debt Collection and Interest Rate Reduction Schemes* (Sept. 10, 2013), *available at* http://www.ftc.gov/news-events/press-releases/2013/09/ftc-settlement-bans-defendants-engaging-debt-collection-and.

[57] *FTC v. Pinnacle Payment Sys., LLC*, No. 1:13-CV-3455 (N.D. Ga. Oct. 21, 2013) (ex parte TRO); *see also* Press Release, *At the FTC's Request, Court Halts Collection of Allegedly Fake Payday Debts* (Oct. 24, 2013), *available at* http://www.ftc.gov/news-events/press-releases/2013/10/ftcs-request-court-halts-collection-allegedly-fake-payday-debts.

Pinnacle is the FTC's fifth recent case involving allegedly fraudulent, online payday-loan-related operations.[58] Litigation in this matter is ongoing.

Medical Debt Collection

In addition to its law enforcement actions described above, the Commission's enforcement work has included an investigation of a company's conduct involving on-site medical debt collection, whereby debt collectors seek payments from consumers while they are receiving treatment at a medical facility.

The Commission recently reviewed evidence that Accretive Health, Inc. ("Accretive") employed debt collectors to collect defaulted debts in hospital emergency rooms and other sensitive hospital areas. While staff ultimately closed its investigation of Accretive's debt collection practices,[59] the Division of Financial Practices issued a letter highlighting some of the concerns raised by on-site medical debt collection. For example, collection attempts in such circumstances may deter consumers from seeking necessary medical care because consumers fear that they will be confronted with debts that they do not have the means to pay. Some consumers may even fear that the hospital may withhold necessary treatment unless payments are made. Such collection attempts also could interfere with the provision of medical treatment, either by delaying treatment while the collection attempt is made, or by adding additional emotional stress for the patient. Moreover, consumers are not normally well-positioned in such circumstances to evaluate the validity of the alleged debt and their financial ability to make any payments. For example, consumers will not normally have access to their paperwork and records, or the status of their financial resources, while awaiting medical treatment in an

---

[58] Other recent FTC matters involving allegedly fraudulent online payday-loan-related operations include *Pro Credit, Inc.* (M.D. Fla. 2013), *Caprice Mktg. LLC* (N.D. Ill. 2013), *American Credit Crunchers, LLC* (N.D. Ill. 2012), and *Broadway Global Master Inc.* (E.D. Cal. 2012).

[59] The FTC, however, did enter into a consent agreement with Accretive to resolve complaint allegations relating to the company's data security practices. *See* Accretive Health, Inc., No. C-4432 (Feb. 5, 2014); *see also* Press Release, *FTC Approves Final Consent Settling Charges that Accretive Health Failed to Adequately Protect Consumers' Personal Information* (Feb. 24, 2014), *available at* http://www.ftc.gov/news-events/press-releases/2014/02/ftc-approves-final-consent-settling-charges-accretive-health.

emergency room. Thus, debt collectors or other entities that engage in this activity may violate the FDCPA and the FTC Act.

The Commission staff closed its investigation of Accretive because, while there was evidence that Accretive had used unlawful debt collection practices in the State of Minnesota, staff's investigation had yielded very little evidence that such tactics were employed by Accretive in other parts of the country. In deciding not to recommend enforcement action against Accretive at this time, FTC staff noted that Accretive already has been banned from collection activity in Minnesota pursuant to a settlement with the State's Attorney General that also required Accretive to pay $2.5 million.

5.3 Debt collection advocacy

5.3.1 Joint CFPB-FTC amicus briefs

In the past year, the Bureau and the FTC have appeared together as amici (friends of the court) in two cases arising under the FDCPA.

Delgado v. Capital Management Services (7th Cir.)

The Bureau joined the FTC in filing an amicus brief in this private class action lawsuit in August 2013.[60] The case concerns the practice by some debt collectors of attempting to collect "time-barred debts," debts for which the statute of limitations for initiating a collection action has expired. Once the statute of limitations has passed, the debt collector no longer has the right to sue the consumer to collect the debt. The debt collector in this case sent the plaintiff a dunning letter with a limited-time offer to settle a debt for which the statute of limitations had expired. The district court declined to dismiss the case, holding that it was plausible that an unsophisticated consumer could be deceived into believing that the offer of settlement implies a legally enforceable obligation to pay the debt.

---

[60] Brief of Amici Curiae, *Delgado v. Capital Mgmt. Servs., LP*, No. 13-2030 (7th Cir. Aug. 14, 2013).

The debt collector appealed the district court's decision to the U.S. Court of Appeals for the Seventh Circuit ("Seventh Circuit"), which invited the FTC to file an amicus brief. The FTC's amicus brief, which was joined by the Bureau, observed that, in some circumstances, a debt collector may seek voluntary payment of a time-barred debt without violating the FDCPA. However, the brief argued that the FDCPA may be violated if the debt collector engages in communication that deceives or misleads unsophisticated consumers. Although such deception may occur if the communication involves filing or threatening litigation to collect a time-barred debt, the brief argued that the FDCPA may be also violated if the debt collector engages in other types of deceptive or misleading communications.

On March 11, 2014, the Seventh Circuit issued a decision consistent with the agencies' position.[61] Specifically, the court held that the FDCPA is violated "if the debt collector uses language in its dunning letter that would mislead an unsophisticated consumer into believing that the debt is legally enforceable, regardless of whether the letter actually threatens litigation."[62]

Sykes v. Mel S. Harris & Associates, LLC (2d. Cir.)

The Bureau and the FTC filed an amicus brief in this private class action lawsuit in November 2013.[63] The Bureau appeared as amicus curiae in the oral argument in the case in February 2014. The case raises important issues regarding the practices of debt buyers who purchase defaulted debts, use aggressive and improper litigation tactics to obtain default judgments against consumers, and use those default judgments to freeze bank accounts and garnish wages.

Plaintiffs here brought suit against a group of affiliated debt-buying companies, their outside law firm and certain of its attorneys, and a process serving agency and its attorneys. Plaintiffs allege that defendants used tactics like "sewer service"[64] and false court affidavits to obtain

---

[61] *McMahon v. LVNV Funding, LLC* and *Delgado v. Capital Management Services*, Nos. 12-3504,13-2030, 2014 WL 929358 (7th Cir. March 11, 2014).

[62] *Id.* at *9.

[63] Brief of Amici Curiae, *Sykes v. Mel S. Harris & Assoc. LLC*, No. 13-2742 (2nd Cir. November 13, 2013).

[64] "Sewer service" refers to the intentional failure to provide service of process on a named party of a lawsuit.

default judgments against consumers in over 120,000 debt collection actions over a three-year period in New York City civil court.

Defendants have urged that they are essentially immune from FDCPA liability because all of their false statements were directed at the State courts, and not consumers. The agencies' amicus brief explains that such a limitation finds no basis in the language of the FDCPA, and that such a result would be contrary to the Act's overarching consumer-protection purposes.

The U.S. Court of Appeals for the Second Circuit heard oral argument on the matter on February 7, 2014, and the Bureau presented its views to the court. The court has not issued a decision.

6. Education and outreach initiatives

The Bureau empowers consumers to make sound financial decisions for themselves and their families through wide-ranging consumer education efforts. These efforts include outreach to targeted consumer populations, including students, older Americans, servicemembers and veterans, and low-income and economically-vulnerable consumers. Similarly, the FTC's FDCPA program also involves extensive education and public outreach efforts. The FTC's consumer education informs consumers of their rights under the FDCPA and what the statute requires of debt collectors, while its business education informs debt collectors what they must do to comply with the law.

6.1 Bureau education and outreach initiatives

The Bureau creates an interactive, informative relationship between consumers and the Bureau to link consumers to information about specific financial decisions, including those relating to debt collection, and to help inform the Bureau's policymaking. One of the Bureau's initiatives is Ask CFPB, an interactive online tool that helps consumers find short, clear, unbiased, authoritative answers to their financial questions.

Ask CFPB for debt collections was initiated in October 2012. As of January 2014, there were more than 85 debt collection questions with answers provided in Ask CFPB. Debt collection was the fourth most-viewed category. The Ask CFPB questions and answers on debt collection address a wide range of issues under the FDCPA, including the meaning of specific terms, consumers' rights, and debt collectors' obligations. The questions and answers address many specific debt collection topics, as well as other Federal and State laws that may apply to debt collection practices. Ask CFPB provides practical tips to consumers regarding steps they can take to exercise their rights under the FDCPA or better manage their debts.

Ask CFPB also includes FAQs targeted to special consumer populations. For example, one segment of the debt collection FAQs addresses issues related to a survivor's obligations with respect to the debt of someone who is deceased, which may be particularly relevant to widows and widowers who may be older adults. There are also segments of the FAQs that address collection of student loans debts, as well as the rights, obligations, and specific circumstances of servicemembers and their families.

On May 15, 2013, the Bureau launched its Spanish language website (consumerfinance.gov/es), which also features Ask CFPB in Spanish. CFPB en Español currently includes more than 40 Spanish language questions and answers on debt collection.

In July 2013, the Bureau added five sample letters to Ask CFPB that consumers may use when they interact with debt collectors. These letters can help consumers get valuable information and protect them from inappropriate or unwanted collection activities. The five letters address the following situations: (1) consumers who need more information about a debt; (2) consumers who want to dispute their debt; (3) consumers who want to restrict how and when a collector can contact them; (4) consumers who have hired an attorney with respect to the debt matter; and (5) consumers who want to stop all communication from debt collectors. Copies of these letters are available on the Bureau's website at http://www.consumerfinance.gov/askcfpb/1695/ive-been-contacted-debt-collector-and-need-help-responding-how-do-i-reply.html.

Debt collection is a significant issue facing consumers, especially low-income and economically-vulnerable consumers. Therefore, the Bureau is coordinating with certain law school clinics, which can be a key resource for economically vulnerable consumers confronting legal issues around consumer financial products and services.

Empowering consumers to handle their student loan debts has been and will continue to be a significant focus for the Bureau. The Bureau has released a web tool, Repay Student Debt,[65] for borrowers who have fallen behind on their student loan payments. The tool has helped borrowers understand their options, communicate effectively with their loan servicer or debt collector, and work to bring their loans out of default or delinquency. Improving their performance in paying student loan debts helps borrowers to rebuild their credit, go back to school, or buy a home.[66]

6.2 FTC education and public outreach

The Commission educates consumers through English and Spanish print and online materials, one-on-one guidance, blog posts, and speeches and presentations. To maximize its outreach efforts, FTC staff works with an informal network of about 10,000 community-based organizations and other interest groups that order FTC products and distribute FTC information to their members, clients, and constituents. Most of the 10 million or so print publications the FTC distributes each year are disseminated through these trusted local partners, which include libraries, police departments, schools, non-profit organizations, banks, credit unions and other corporations, and government agencies. Staff offers instructions on how to share FTC materials by linking, reprinting, and co-branding. In addition, the FTC logs more than 28 million accesses of its publications online every year. The FTC's channel at YouTube.com/FTCVideos houses more than 80 videos, which were viewed nearly one million times in 2013.

---

[65] *Available at* http://www.consumerfinance.gov/paying-for-college/repay-student-debt/#Question-1.

[66] For borrowers with private student loans, options to cure a student loan in default may be limited. In May 2013, the Bureau published *Student Loan Affordability*, a report analyzing 28,000 comments from policy experts, market participants, and consumers offering potential options for policymakers seeking to help borrowers manage their student debt. *Available at* http://www.consumerfinance.gov/reports/student-loan-affordability/. *Student Loan Affordability* featured a discussion of possible options for borrowers in distress, including increased access to loan modifications for borrowers seeking to avoid default and a mechanism through which private student loan borrowers in default can successfully repair their credit.

In 2013, the Commission supplemented its distribution of information by launching its Financial Educators Site. The site addresses personal finance topics, including: credit and debt, saving and shopping, housing, work and school, and automobiles. Users are encouraged to share the FTC's resources with students, friends, family, coworkers, and neighbors, and to print, copy, post, and link to the materials freely.

The Commission educates industry by developing and distributing business education materials, delivering speeches, participating in panel discussions at industry conferences, and providing interviews to general media and trade publications. A complete list of the FTC's consumer and business education materials relating to debt collection and information on the extent of its distribution is set forth in Appendix A to the FTC's letter.

7. Rulemaking, research, and policy initiatives

The Bureau and FTC engage in research to better understand the marketplace and to inform policymaking initiatives designed to best protect consumers. This research, as well as the continued dialogue and collaboration between the Bureau and FTC, were instrumental in identifying and analyzing information in connection with the Bureau's development and issuance of a debt collection Advance Notice of Proposed Rulemaking ("ANPR") in November 2013.

7.1 Bureau rulemaking, research, and policy development activities

The Bureau engages in research and interacts with key debt collection stakeholders to improve its understanding of the market and to develop policies that will protect consumers without imposing unnecessary or undue costs on industry.

7.1.1 Bureau research and policy development

In June 2013, the Bureau and the FTC held a joint FTC-CFPB Roundtable on data integrity and information flows in debt collection.[67] This joint event, entitled *Life of a Debt: Data Integrity in Debt Collection*, focused on several aspects of information flow in debt collection, including:

---

[67] Additional information about the Roundtable is available at http://www.ftc.gov/bcp/workshops/lifeofadebt.

(1) the amount of documentation and other information currently available to different types of collectors and at different points in the debt collection process; (2) the information needed to verify and substantiate debts; (3) the costs and benefits of providing consumers with additional disclosures about their debts and debt-related rights; and (4) information issues relating to debt collection litigation. The event brought together consumer advocates, credit issuers, collection industry members, State and Federal regulators, and academics to discuss a range of issues, including the documentation required for debt verification and litigation, as well as the costs and benefits of providing additional disclosures to consumers.

In addition, in July 2013, the Bureau held a public field hearing in Portland, Maine to discuss debt collection practices. The hearing included remarks by Director Cordray and others from the Bureau's Research, Markets, and Regulations division. The hearing also included a panel discussion with consumer groups, industry representatives, and academic and financial experts.

CFPB staff also spoke at both national and regional association conferences (e.g., Debt Buyers Association, The Association of Credit and Collections Professionals, The National Association of Retail Collection Attorneys, Consumer Bankers Association, Mid-Atlantic Collectors Association, Northeast Debt Collection Expo, Debt Collection Symposium & Expo, hosted by Resource Management Services, and the Credit & Collections News Credit Grantor Consortium). CFPB staff also addressed consumer advocacy groups at national conferences (e.g., Consumer Action and Consumer Federation of America).

The CFPB further held meetings with many individuals, industry groups, consumer groups, vendors, and government officials to better understand the debt collection industry and ecosystem. In particular, the CFPB met with many of these stakeholders to understand their issues and positions to inform any future rule writing.

7.1.2 Bureau release of an Advanced Notice of Proposed Rulemaking

In November 2013, the Bureau took a crucial first step toward considering consumer protection rules for the debt collection market through the issuance of an ANPR. As the first Federal agency with the authority to write comprehensive rules for debt collectors, the ANPR provides a critical opportunity to obtain information to inform a rulemaking process that will allow the Bureau to address some of the ongoing consumer protection issues in the debt collection market, including those arising from changes in the collections marketplace since the FDCPA was enacted in 1977.[68] The Bureau developed its ANPR based on information from a variety of sources, including ongoing interaction with industry and consumer groups and the Bureau's continuing supervision, enforcement, and consumer education activities. The Bureau's ongoing collaboration with the FTC, including the joint FTC-CFPB Roundtable concerning data integrity and information flow, also provided key insights and information in the development of the ANPR. The ANPR provides the Bureau with an avenue to collect information on a wide array of issues, including the accuracy of information used by debt collectors, consumers' knowledge of their rights, and the communication methods collectors employ to recover debts.

Specifically, the ANPR includes questions that are intended to help the Bureau learn more about several areas of concern:

- First, the ANPR seeks comment on information accuracy issues. In particular, the Bureau wants to learn more about the transfer of information from an original creditor to third-party debt collection firms and debt buyers, and from those parties to other debt collectors and credit bureaus. The Bureau believes that ensuring the integrity of information within the debt collection system is critically important.

- Second, the ANPR examines how best to ensure that consumers have a clear understanding of their rights in the debt collection process. The Bureau believes that it is important that disclosures and information provided to consumers are not confusing, incomplete, or ineffective.

- Finally, the ANPR considers how best to ensure that all collectors treat all consumers fairly and with respect, another key Bureau objective relating to debt collection.

In addition to these broad categories, the ANPR asks specific questions about whether consumers receive and understand validation notices and whether the dispute process can be improved. The Bureau also sought information about an array of communications-related topics, such as possible requirements for the type of messages left by collectors on answering machines or possible requirements related to collection calls placed to mobile phones.

---

[68] The Bureau's ANPR can be found at http://files.consumerfinance.gov/f/201311_cfpb_anpr_debtcollection.pdf.

The comment period for the ANPR ended on February 28, 2014, and the Bureau received more than 20,000 responses. In addition to these comments, Cornell University also submitted a report from RegulationRoom.org, which is operated by law students and staff at Cornell Law School. Cornell's report was based on one thousand responses submitted through RegulationRoom.org. This website makes it easy for people to submit responses to government agencies in an interactive and intuitive way.

The public comments, as well as the Regulation Room report, will provide the Bureau with critical information on the issues described above and lay the groundwork for important next steps with respect to any proposed rule that the Bureau issues under the FDCPA.

7.2 FTC research and policy development activities

In addition to law enforcement and consumer education, the Commission's FDCPA program includes research and policy initiatives. In the past year, the FTC has continued to monitor and evaluate the debt collection industry and its practices. Specifically, as described above, the FTC collaborated with the CFPB to examine the role of data integrity and information flow in debt collection, and provided the Bureau with input on debt collection rulemaking and guidance initiatives.

8. Conclusion

The Bureau will continue to develop its debt collection program over the coming year, and will work actively to protect consumers from the unfair, deceptive, abusive, and other unlawful conduct of some debt collectors. The Bureau looks forward to performing this work in close cooperation with the FTC.

The cases discussed below represent a concerted effort by the FTC to target unlawful debt collection practices including false threats, harassment or abuse, and attempts to collect on "phantom" payday loan debts.

1.   Deceptive, Unfair, and Abusive Collector Conduct

Targeting debt collectors that engage in deceptive, unfair, or abusive conduct continues to be one of the Commission's highest priorities. In particular, the Commission continues to actively pursue debt collectors that secure payments from consumers by falsely threatening litigation or otherwise falsely implying that they are involved in law enforcement. In 2013, the Commission filed or resolved seven actions alleging deceptive, unfair, or abusive debt collection conduct.

In *FTC v. Forensic Case Management Services, Inc.*, the FTC secured substantial monetary judgments against a debt collection enterprise and a complete ban on future debt collection activity, along with other injunctive relief.[4] The FTC's complaint alleged that the defendants violated the FTC Act and the FDCPA through such egregious conduct as threats of physical harm, obscene and profane language, revealing consumers' debts to third parties, and falsely threatening consumers with lawsuits, arrest, and wage garnishment. The judgments in the case exceed $35.5 million, and despite partial suspension based on the defendants' inability to pay, the Commission collected more than $1.1 million for consumer redress.

In *United States v. Expert Global Solutions, Inc.*, the Commission secured a $3.2 million civil penalty for unlawful collection practices —the highest penalty the FTC has ever obtained against a third-party debt collector.[5] The FTC's complaint charged that the company, operating under several business names including "NCO," violated the FDCPA and the FTC Act by employing harassing collection calls, disclosing consumers' debts to third parties, and continuing collection efforts without verifying debts even after consumers said they did not owe those debts. The settlement prohibits the company from engaging in this unlawful conduct and further requires that whenever a consumer disputes the validity or the amount of a debt, the company must either terminate collection efforts or suspend collection until it conducts a reasonable investigation and verifies that its information about the debt is accurate and complete.

---

[4] *FTC v. Forensic Case Mgmt. Servs., Inc.*, No. 2:11-cv-07484 (C.D. Cal. Jan. 4, 2013) (Final Judgment and Order for Permanent Injunction and Monetary Relief), *see also* Press Release, FTC Settlement Obtains Permanent Ban Against Abusive Debt Collection Operation (Jan. 17, 2013), *available at* http://www.ftc.gov/news-events/press-releases/2013/01/ftc-settlement-obtains-permanent-ban-against-abusive-debt.

[5] *United States v. Expert Global Solutions, Inc.*, No. 3:13-cv-2611 (N.D. Tex. July 16, 2013) (Stipulated Order for Permanent Injunction and Monetary Judgment); *see also* Press Release, World's Largest Debt Collection Operation Settles FTC Charges, Will Pay $3.2 Million Penalty (July 9, 2013), *available at* http://www.ftc.gov/news-events/press-releases/2013/07/worlds-largest-debt-collection-operation-settles-ftc-charges-will.

In *United States v. National Attorney Collection Services, Inc.*, the Commission brought its first enforcement action involving the use of text messages to collect debts.[6] The Commission's complaint alleged that the company sent consumers English- and Spanish-language text messages that falsely portrayed the company as a law firm and failed to disclose that it was a debt collector. The company also illegally revealed debts to consumers' family members, friends, and co-workers through the use of mailing envelopes that pictured a large arm shaking money from a consumer being held upside down. The settlement imposed a $1 million civil penalty, requires the company to obtain consumers' express consent before contacting them by text message, and bars the company from making deceptive legal threats, falsely holding itself out to be a law firm, revealing debts to third parties, and omitting required disclosures.

The Commission also obtained an *ex parte* temporary restraining order and other extraordinary relief to shut down a debt collection enterprise permeated by unlawful conduct. In *FTC v. Asset & Capital Management Group*, a U.S. district court entered a temporary restraining order with an asset freeze, receivership, and immediate access to the business premises against a debt collector that the FTC alleged extorted payments from consumers by using false threats of lawsuits and calculated campaigns to embarrass consumers by unlawfully communicating with family members, friends, and coworkers.[7] The FTC's complaint also alleged that the company failed to notify consumers of their right to dispute and obtain verification of their debts, and that its collectors failed to disclose the name of the company they represented, and that they were attempting to collect a debt, during calls to consumers. The Commission continues to litigate the *Asset & Capital Management* matter.

In *FTC v. Security Credit Services, LLC*, the Commission alleged that a debt collection enterprise falsely threatened consumers with lawsuits and misled consumers into paying unnecessary fees.[8] The FTC's complaint alleges that the company violated the FTC Act and the FDCPA by deceiving consumers into using a payment method that required a substantial "convenience fee." In addition, while one defendant in this case was a law firm that in some instances sued consumers for nonpayment, the complaint alleges that the firm regularly threatened to sue consumers where it did not have the authority to do so or in jurisdictions where it was not licensed to practice law, in violation of the FDCPA. The settlement in this case stops the false threats of suit and secures nearly $800,000 in restitution for consumers for deceptively-obtained convenience fees.

---

[6] Complaint, *United States v. Nat'l Attorney Collection Servs., Inc.*, No. 2:13-cv-6212 (C.D. Cal. Aug. 23, 2013); *see also* Press Release, FTC Brings First Case Alleging Text Messages Were Used In Illegal Debt Collection Scheme (Sept. 25, 2013), *available at* http://www.ftc.gov/news-events/press-releases/2013/09/ftc-brings-first-case-alleging-text-messages-were-used-illegal.

[7] *FTC v. Asset & Capital Mgmt. Grp., LLC*, No. CV13-5267 (C.D. Cal. July 24, 2013) (*ex parte* TRO); *see also* Press Release, At FTC's Request, Court Orders Halt to Debt Collector's Illegal Practices, Freezes Assets (Aug. 1, 2013), *available at* http://www.ftc.gov/news-events/press-releases/2013/08/ftcs-request-court-orders-halt-debt-collectors-illegal-practices.

[8] *FTC v. Security Credit Services, LLC*, No. 1:13-cv-799 (N.D. Ga. Mar. 19, 2013) (Stipulated Final Judgment and Order for Permanent Injunction); *see also* Press Release, In Settlement with FTC, Debt Collectors Agree to Stop Deceiving Consumers and Pay Nearly $800,000 (Mar. 26, 2013), *available at* http://www.ftc.gov/news-events/press-releases/2013/03/settlement-ftc-debt-collectors-agree-stop-deceiving-consumers-and.

Finally, the FTC recently settled allegations in *FTC v. AMG Services, Inc.* that a payday lender, collecting on its own behalf, violated the FTC Act by falsely threatening to take legal action against consumers.[9] The Commission also obtained a temporary restraining order with an asset freeze in *FTC v. Goldman Schwartz*—a case alleging that the defendant falsely threatened consumers with arrest, disclosed consumers' debts to third parties, collected unauthorized fees, engaged in harassing and abusive conduct, failed to provide required notices, and made collection calls before 8:00 a.m. and after 9:00 p.m.[10]

2. Phantom Debt Collection

One of the Commission's major consumer protection concerns is the continuing rise of so-called "phantom debt collectors." Phantom debt collectors engage in unfair, deceptive, or abusive conduct by attempting to collect on debts that either do not exist or are not owed to the phantom debt collector. In the past year, the Commission has filed or resolved two actions against phantom debt collectors.

In September 2013, in *FTC v. Pro Credit Group, LLC*, a U.S district court entered a set of stipulated permanent injunctions and judgments totaling $67.5 million against the defendants for violations of the FTC Act and the Commission's Telemarketing Sales Rule, 16 C.F.R. Part 310.[11] The complaint alleged that the defendants, working closely with an overseas call center in India, defrauded consumers out of millions of dollars by collecting payments for debts that the consumers did not owe to them or did not owe at all. The victims of this scam include consumers who previously applied for or received loans from online payday loan companies and supplied sensitive personal financial information in the process—information that eventually made its way to the defendants. The settlements ban defendants from engaging in telemarketing, debt collection, debt relief services, and/or the sale of financial-related goods or services, depending on the individual defendant's role in the enterprise. The settlement also includes an unsuspended judgment of approximately $25 million against one of the individual defendants, and while monetary judgments against the other defendants were largely suspended based on inability to pay, defendants were all required to turn over cash on hand, real estate, and other significant assets.

---

[9] *FTC v. AMG Services, Inc.*, No. 2:12-cv-536 (D. Nev. July 18, 2013) (Agreed Joint Motion to Enter Stipulated Order for Permanent Injunction and Judgment); *see also* Press Release, AMG Defendants Settle FTC's Debt Collection Charges (July 22, 2013), *available at* http://www.ftc.gov/news-events/press-releases/2013/07/amg-defendants-settle-ftc's-debt-collection-charges. The Commission continues to litigate other aspects of its case against AMG Services.

[10] Complaint, *FTC v. Goldman Schwartz*, No. 4:13-cv-106 (S.D. Tex. Jan. 31, 2013); *see also* Press Release, FTC Action Leads to Shutdown of Texas-based Debt Collector that Allegedly Used Deception, Insults, and False Threats Against Consumers (Jan. 31, 2013), *available at* http://www.ftc.gov/opa/2013/01/goldman.shtm.

[11] *FTC v. Pro Credit Grp., LLC*, No. 8:12-cv-586 (M.D. Fla. Sept. 5, 2013) (stipulated final judgments as to all remaining defendants); *see also* Press Release, FTC Settlement Bans Defendants from Engaging in Debt Collection and Interest Rate Reduction Schemes (Sept. 10, 2013), *available at* http://www.ftc.gov/news-events/press-releases/2013/09/ftc-settlement-bans-defendants-engaging-debt-collection-and.

In *FTC v. Pinnacle Payment Services, LLC*, the Commission charged that defendants, working out of offices in Atlanta and Cleveland, collected and processed millions of dollars in payment for phantom debts using robocalls and voice messages that threatened legal action and arrest unless consumers responded within a few days.[12] Callers also often claimed an affiliation with a law firm or a law enforcement agency. The Commission obtained an *ex parte* temporary restraining order with an asset freeze, receivership, and immediate access against the defendants, and the court hearing the matter recently entered a preliminary injunction. *Pinnacle* is the FTC's second phantom debt collection action this year, and its fifth recent case involving allegedly fraudulent, online payday-loan-related operations.[13] Litigation in this matter is ongoing.

B.   Other Law Enforcement Activities

1.   Time-Barred Debt: *Delgado* Amicus Brief

An ongoing issue in debt collection concerns the collection of debt that is beyond the applicable statute of limitations (also known as "time-barred debt"). Although a past-statute debt remains a valid obligation owed by the consumer in every state except Mississippi and Wisconsin, consumers have a dispositive affirmative defense to any legal action initiated to collect a past-statute debt.[14] For this reason, as many jurisdictions have recognized, threatening to file a lawsuit to collect on a past-statute debt is a violation of the law.[15]

---

[12] *FTC v. Pinnacle Payment Sys., LLC*, No. 1:13-CV-3455 (N.D. Ga. Oct. 21, 2013) (*ex parte* TRO); *see also* Press Release, At the FTC's Request, Court Halts Collection of Allegedly Fake Payday Debts (Oct. 24, 2013), *available at* http://www.ftc.gov/news-events/press-releases/2013/10/ftcs-request-court-halts-collection-allegedly-fake-payday-debts.

[13] Other recent FTC matters involving allegedly fraudulent online payday-loan-related operations include *Pro Credit, Inc.* (M.D. Fla. 2013), *Caprice Mktg. LLC* (N.D. Ill. 2013), *American Credit Crunchers, LLC* (N.D. Ill. 2012), and *Broadway Global Master Inc.* (E.D. Cal. 2012).

[14] California has recently gone further with regard to debt buyers, prohibiting them from filing suit or initiating arbitration if the applicable statute of limitations on their claim has expired. Fair Debt Buying Practices Act, CAL. CIV. CODE §§ 1788.56 (West 2014).

[15] *See United States v. Asset Acceptance LLC*, 8:12-cv-182 (M.D. Fla. Jan. 30, 2012) (stipulated order in case alleging that debt buyer failed to disclose that debts were too old to be legally enforceable); *Baptist v. Global Holding & Inv. Co., LLC*, CIV No. 04-CV-2365 (DGT), 2007 WL 1989450, at *5-6 (E.D.N.Y. July 9, 2007) (finding threat to sue on time-barred debt was a deceptive practice that violated Section 807 of the FDCPA); *Kimber v. Fed. Fin. Corp.*, 668 F. Supp. 1480, 1489 (M.D. Ala. 1987) (holding that a threat to sue on a time-bared debt violated Section 807 of the FDCPA because the collector "implicitly represented that it could recover in a lawsuit, when it fact it cannot properly do so"). Several states also require debt buyers and/or debt collectors to provide a disclosure when collecting on time-barred debts. *See, e.g.*, Fair Debt Buying Practices Act, CAL. CIV. CODE §§ 1788.52-.64 (West 2014); 940 MASS. CODE REGS. 7.07(24) (2014); N.M. CODE R. § 12.2.12.9 (LexisNexis 2014); *see also* FTC, REPAIRING A BROKEN SYSTEM: PROTECTING CONSUMERS IN DEBT COLLECTION LITIGATION AND ARBITRATION 25-28 (2010) [hereinafter REPAIRING A BROKEN SYSTEM], *available at* http://www.ftc.gov/os/2010/07/debtcollectionreport.pdf.

In the 2011 case *United States v. Asset Acceptance, LLC*, the Commission alleged that, in attempting to collect on debts that it knew or should have known were time-barred, Asset Acceptance created the misleading impression that it could sue consumers if they did not pay.[16] The Commission alleged that Asset Acceptance's failure to disclose to consumers that it could not legally sue them if they did not pay was a deceptive practice violating Section 5 of the FTC Act. In a stipulated settlement to remedy this alleged violation, Asset Acceptance agreed to disclose that it will not sue to collect on any debt that it knows or should know is time-barred.

In August 2013, the Commission and the CFPB filed a joint amicus brief in response to an invitation from the Seventh Circuit to present the Commission's views on the application of the FDCPA to the collection of debts barred by the statute of limitations.[17] In the underlying case, a debt collector sent the plaintiff a dunning letter with a limited-time offer to settle a time-barred debt. The plaintiff's ensuing class-action suit against the debt collector contends that this letter violates the FDCPA's prohibition on the use of "any false, deceptive, or misleading representation or means in connection with the collection of any debt."[18] The collector moved to dismiss the suit, arguing that, as a matter of law, the letter could not have violated the FDCPA because it was not an explicit or implied threat to sue.

The joint brief notes that several courts have previously held that a collector who sues or threatens suit on a time-barred debt violates the FDCPA, and argues that, depending on the circumstances, a time-limited settlement offer could plausibly mislead a consumer to believe a debt is enforceable in court even if the offer is unaccompanied by any clearly implied threat of litigation. The brief makes clear that a debt collector may seek voluntary payment of a time-barred debt without violating the FDCPA, even if its collection communications are silent as to the statute of limitations. The brief argues, however, that actual or threatened litigation is not a necessary predicate for an FDCPA violation in the context of time-barred debt; rather, a debt collector violates the statute whenever its communications tend to deceive or mislead "unsophisticated consumers" into believing that a time-barred debt could be the subject of a collection suit.

The Seventh Circuit heard oral argument on the matter in September 2013, but has not yet issued a decision.

---

[16] *United States v. Asset Acceptance, LLC*, No. 8:12-cv-182 (M.D. Fla. Jan. 31, 2012) (order entering consent decree); *see also* Press Release, Under FTC Settlement, Debt Buyer Agrees to Pay $2.5 Million for Alleged Consumer Deception (Jan. 30, 2012), *available at* http://www.ftc.gov/opa/2012/01/asset.shtm.

[17] Brief of Amici Curiae, *Delgado v. Capital Mgmt. Servs., LP*, No. 13-2030 (7th Cir. Aug. 14, 2013), *available at* http://www.ftc.gov/policy/advocacy/amicus-briefs/2013/08/juanita-delgado-v-capital-management-services-lp. The court invited the Commission to file a brief because the district court, in reaching its decision, had relied on the FTC's 2013 report entitled "The Structure and Practice of the Debt Buying Industry."

[18] FDCPA § 807, 15 U.S.C. § 1692e.

2.   Scope of FDCPA Coverage: *Sykes* Amicus Brief

In November 2013, the Commission joined the CFPB in filing an amicus brief in the Second Circuit urging the Court to find that false communications or other deceptive or unfair conduct in connection with the collection of debt is actionable under the FDCPA even if it occurs as part of a legal pleading.[19] In the underlying case, class-action plaintiffs allege that the defendants, who regularly sued consumers for non-payment of debt, knew or should have known that their process servers frequently failed to serve the consumers with notice of suit. When consumers did not respond to these lawsuits, defendants allegedly sought default judgments by submitting affidavits swearing they had personal knowledge that process had been served. Plaintiffs' suit claims that defendants' debt collection practices amount to the knowing authorization of false affidavits to mislead the courts and the consumers, and that such practices violate the FDCPA's prohibition against deceptive or unfair collection methods. In response, defendants contend that the FDCPA does not apply to "communications made either to third parties not affiliated with the debtors that the statute seeks to protect, or in circumstances otherwise having no chance of debtor deception."

In our joint amicus brief, the Bureau and the Commission make clear that the FDCPA broadly prohibits deceptive and unfair collection practices in any form. The brief argues that false affidavits in debt collection suits are directed at consumers, since defendant-consumers are required to be served with such affidavits and since it is the consumers who are ultimately injured by this fraud on the court. Even assuming *arguendo*, however, that defendants' misconduct was directed at the court and not consumers, the FDCPA does not provide any textual basis for excluding conduct that is only meant to deceive or mislead a state court or other party. The brief points to 15 U.S.C. Section 1692e of the Act, which states that "[a] debt collector may not use *any* false, deceptive, or misleading representation or means *in connection with* the collection of any debt" (emphasis added), as well as to Section 1692f, which prohibits collectors from using "unfair or unconscionable means to collect or attempt to collect any debt" without limitation.[20] The brief asks the Court to "apply the text of the FDCPA as Congress has written it, without limiting its plain scope based on defendants' incorrect assessment of the Act's purposes," and "accordingly reject defendants' attempt to read into the Act a blanket immunity for conduct that is 'directed at' third parties."

The Second Circuit heard oral argument on the matter on February 7, 2014, but has not yet issued a decision.

---

[19] Brief of Amici Curiae, *Sykes v. Mel S. Harris & Assocs. LLC*, No. 13-2742 (2d Cir. Nov. 13, 2013), *available at* http://www.ftc.gov/policy/advocacy/amicus-briefs/2013/11/sykes-v-mel-s-harris-associates-llc.

[20] FDCPA §§ 807, 808, 15 U.S.C. §§ 1692e, 1692f.

3.   Required Remote Tribal Arbitration: *Jackson* Amicus Brief

The Commission has taken a particular interest in stemming the consumer harm that can flow from unlawful arbitration tactics. In its recent report on protecting consumers in debt collection litigation and arbitration, the Commission noted that mandatory pre-dispute arbitration clauses have become increasingly common in consumer contracts for goods and services. The Commission emphasized that such arbitration should be permitted only if creditors provide consumers with meaningful choice as to whether their disputes will be arbitrated, and that any arbitration should be conducted with an emphasis on making it more likely that consumers can appear and participate.[21]

In *FTC v. Payday Financial, LLC*, the Commission continues to litigate against online payday lenders that regularly file collection actions against borrowers in remote tribal courts, alleging that this practice is deceptive and unfair in violation of Section 5 of the FTC Act.[22] Though the FTC's case against Payday Financial challenges the defendants' litigation practices as opposed to arbitration practices, the Commission learned a great deal about the defendants' arbitration practices during discovery. In July 2012, during the pendency of the Commission's *Payday Financial* litigation, a private action involving the same defendants and similar charges reached the Court of Appeals for the Seventh Circuit. In September 2013, in response to an invitation from the Seventh Circuit, the Commission filed an amicus brief expressing its views on the validity of the *Payday Financial* defendants' arbitration clauses, which purport to require borrowers to resolve all payday loan-related disputes through arbitration conducted on a reservation of the Cheyenne River Sioux Tribe in South Dakota.[23]

The amicus brief revisits the FTC's contention that suing consumers in a remote tribal court that lacks jurisdiction is an unfair collection practice under Section 5 of the FTC Act, and then examines how the factors that make this practice unfair under Section 5 may support a similar conclusion in the class action litigation: that requiring tribal arbitration of consumer disputes is unconscionable. In its analysis, the Commission notes that the remoteness of the tribal forum[24] imposes disproportionate financial and informational burdens on financially-distressed consumers, effectively pressuring them to abandon legal claims or defenses—a

---

[21] REPAIRING A BROKEN SYSTEM at iv-v, 40-41.

[22] Amended Complaint, *FTC v. Payday Fin., LLC*, No. 3:11-cv-3017 (D.S.D. Mar. 7, 2012); *see also* Press Release, FTC Charges That Payday Lender Illegally Sued Debt-Burdened Consumers in South Dakota Tribal Court Without Jurisdiction (Mar. 7, 2012), *available at* http://www.ftc.gov/news-events/press-releases/2012/03/ftc-charges-payday-lender-illegally-sued-debt-burdened.

[23] Brief of Amicus Curiae, *Jackson v. Payday Fin., LLC*, No. 12-2617 (7th Cir. Sept. 13, 2013), *available at* http://www.ftc.gov/policy/advocacy/amicus-briefs/2013/09/deborah-jackson-v-payday-financial-llc.

[24] The defendants in this action do not lend either to members of the Cheyenne River Sioux tribe or to residents of South Dakota, and thus all borrowers are non-members of the tribe and reside outside of South Dakota.

substantial injury to those consumers. In addition, false, inconsistent, and confusing representations in the arbitration clauses undermine borrowers' ability to understand these provisions, making such injury not reasonably avoidable by the consumer. The Commission concluded that these issues, taken together, could contribute to a finding that the arbitration clauses are both procedurally and substantively unconscionable.

The Seventh Circuit has not yet conducted oral arguments on the issues addressed by the Commission's brief.

4. Medical Debt Collection: Accretive Health, Inc. Closing Letter

The Commission also continues to be concerned about collection tactics that pressure consumers into abandoning their rights under the FDCPA. A practice that recently exemplified this concern is on-site medical debt collection, whereby debt collectors seek payments from consumers while they are receiving treatment at a medical facility.

The Commission recently reviewed evidence that Accretive Health, Inc. ("Accretive") employed debt collectors to collect defaulted debts in hospital emergency rooms and other sensitive hospital areas. While staff ultimately closed its investigation of Accretive, the Division of Financial Practices issued a letter highlighting some of the concerns raised by on-site medical debt collection.[25] For example, collection attempts in such circumstances may deter consumers from seeking necessary medical care because consumers fear that they will be confronted with debts that they do not have the means to pay. Some consumers may even fear that the hospital may withhold necessary treatment unless payments are made. Such collection attempts also could interfere with the provision of medical treatment, either by delaying treatment while the collection attempt is made, or by adding additional emotional stress for the patient. Moreover, consumers are not normally well-positioned in such circumstances to evaluate the validity of the alleged debt and their financial ability to make any payments. For example, consumers will not normally have access to their paperwork and records, or the status of their financial resources, while awaiting medical treatment in an emergency room. Thus, debt collectors or other entities that engage in this activity may violate the FDCPA and the FTC Act.

The Commission staff closed its investigation of Accretive because, while there was evidence that Accretive had used unlawful debt collection practices in the state of Minnesota, staff's investigation had yielded very little evidence that such tactics were employed by Accretive in other parts of the country. In deciding not to recommend enforcement action against Accretive at this time, FTC staff noted that Accretive already has been banned from collection activity in Minnesota pursuant to a $2.5 million settlement with the state's Attorney General.

---

[25] Letter from FTC's Division of Financial Practices to counsel for Accretive Health, Inc. (Dec. 31, 2013), *available at* http://www.ftc.gov/sites/default/files/documents/closing_letters/fair-debt-collection-practices-act/131231fairdebtclubokletter.pdf.

III.   Education and Public Outreach

The second prong of the Commission's debt collection program is education and public outreach. Consumer education informs consumers of their rights under the FDCPA and what the statute requires of debt collectors. Business education informs debt collectors what they must do to comply with the law. The FTC also engages in public outreach to enhance legal services providers' understanding of debt collection issues.

The Commission educates consumers through English and Spanish print and online materials, one-on-one guidance, blog posts, and speeches and presentations. To maximize its outreach efforts, FTC staff works with an informal network of about 10,000 community-based organizations and other interest groups that order FTC products and distribute FTC information to their members, clients, and constituents. Most of the 10 million or so print publications the FTC distributes each year are disseminated through these trusted local partners, which include libraries, police departments, schools, non-profit organizations, banks, credit unions and other corporations, and government agencies. Staff offers instructions on how to share FTC materials by linking, reprinting, and co-branding. In addition, the FTC logs more than 28 million accesses of its publications online every year. The FTC's channel at YouTube.com/FTCVideos houses more than 80 videos, which were viewed nearly one million times in 2013.

This past year, the Commission supplemented its distribution of information by launching its Financial Educators Site.[26] The site addresses personal finance topics, including: credit and debt; saving and shopping; housing; work and school; and automobiles. Users are encouraged to share our resources with students, friends, family, coworkers, and neighbors, and to print, copy, post, and link to the materials freely.

The Commission educates industry by developing and distributing business education materials, delivering speeches, participating in panel discussions at industry conferences, and providing interviews to general media and trade publications. A complete list of the FTC's consumer and business education materials relating to debt collection and information on the extent of their distribution is set forth in Appendix A to this letter.

As part of the FTC's Legal Services Collaboration project, FTC staff regularly meets with legal services providers to discuss various consumer protection issues, including the FTC's work in the debt collection arena. In 2013, FTC staff provided in-person trainings or presentations that involved debt collection issues throughout the country, including in Austin, Edison (NJ), Lansing (MI), San Francisco, Seattle, and Washington, DC. FTC staff also provided updates about the agency's debt collection work during nationwide webinars hosted by the National Association for Consumer Advocates in March, August, and November of 2013, and in a webinar hosted by the Legal Services Corporation for its grantees in November. Additionally, the FTC organizes "Common Ground" conferences that bring together legal services providers and law enforcement to discuss a wide variety of consumer protection issues,

---

[26] *Financial Educators*, FTC, http://www.consumer.ftc.gov/features/feature-0022-financial-educators.

including debt collection. The agency has held 21 Common Ground conferences over the past several years in cities around the country.

Finally, the FTC worked with ChildFocus, Inc. and the Annie E. Casey Foundation to help produce the free guide, *Youth and Credit: Protecting the Credit of Youth in Foster Care*.[27] This guide discusses credit issues facing the more than 26,000 children in the United States who age out of foster care every year. In 2011, Congress passed legislation to help people in foster care better protect their credit. Now, when foster children turn 16, child welfare agencies are required to get their annual credit reports. The legislation also requires agencies to help children clear up their credit, including debt collection issues resulting from identity theft, so they can better launch their lives as independent young adults. One of the over-arching goals of the guide is youth empowerment: using this opportunity to help young people understand what credit is, why it is important to their future financial stability, and how bad credit can derail their goals. It also gives adults some tools to help children if their identity has been stolen, including resources to help them identify charged-off debts and fix credit fraud and errors.

IV.   Research and Policy Development Activities

The third prong of the Commission's debt collection program is research and policy initiatives. In the past year, the FTC has continued to monitor and evaluate the debt collection industry and its practices. Specifically, as described below, the FTC has collaborated with the CFPB to examine the role of data integrity in debt collection, and has provided the Bureau with input on debt collection rulemaking and guidance initiatives.

A.   Life of a Debt Roundtable Event

Building on the findings of the Commission's seminal study of the debt buying industry,[28] the FTC and the CFPB convened a group of consumer advocates, credit issuers, collection industry members, state and federal regulators, and academics to discuss the flow of consumer data throughout the debt collection process. This joint event, entitled *Life of a Debt: Data Integrity in Debt Collection* and held in June 2013,[29] was open to the public and focused on several aspects of information flow in debt collection, including: (1) the amount of documentation and other information currently available to different types of collectors and at different points in the debt collection process; (2) the information needed to verify and substantiate debts; (3) the costs and benefits of providing consumers with additional disclosures about their debts and debt-related rights; and (4) information issues relating to pleading and judgment in debt collection litigation.

---

[27] This guide is available online at http://www.aecf.org/~/media/Pubs/Topics/Child%20Welfare%20Permanence/Other/YouthandCredit/YouthandCredit.pdf.

[28] FTC, THE STRUCTURE AND PRACTICES OF THE DEBT BUYING INDUSTRY (2013), *available at* http://www.ftc.gov/reports/structure-practices-debt-buying-industry.

[29] Additional information about this event is available on the FTC's website at http://www.ftc.gov/news-events/events-calendar/2013/06/life-debt-data-integrity-debt-collection.

Appendix A
Debt Collection Educational Material Distribution in 2013

Consumer or Business Educational Material	Offline Distribution		Online Access[31]	
	English	**Spanish**	**English**	**Spanish**
Consumer Education: Brochures				
Coping with Debt	75,350	12,250	167,105	1,673
Debt Collection	69,350	3,800	438,899	16,694
Debt Collection Arbitration	25,700	N/A	10,041	524
Consumer Education: Articles on consumer.ftc.gov (Online Only)				
Debts and Deceased Relatives	N/A	N/A	29,524	3,719
Fake Debt Collectors	N/A	N/A	45,120	593
Garnishing Federal Benefits	N/A	N/A	19,556	633
Identity Theft and Debt Collection	N/A	N/A	13,309	640
Settling Credit Card Debt	N/A	N/A	79,264	3,660
Statement of Rights for Identity Theft Victims	N/A	N/A	11,221	501
Stop Calls and Letters from a Debt Collector	N/A	N/A	14,336	657
Time-Barred Debts	N/A	N/A	85,778	4,914
Consumer Education: Video (Online Only)				
Dealing with Debt Collectors	N/A	N/A	16,874	3,970
Helping Victims of Identity Theft	N/A	N/A	6,027	N/A
Bookmarks				
Dealing with Debt	38,100	N/A	1,631	N/A
Business Education: Brochures				
The Fair Debt Collection Practices Act	1,217	N/A	2,980	N/A
Business Education: Video (Online Only)				
Debt Collection	N/A	N/A	6,959	N/A

---

[31] Online access numbers only include access through September 2013, and do not include access to materials that are downloaded from FTC channels and reposted on outside websites.

Additional Debt Collection Educational Material[32]

Consumer Education

Blog Posts:

- The jig is up for bogus debt collection and rate reduction operations

- Haunted by Phantom Debt?

- A Text Twist on Debt Collection

- FTC Launches its New Financial Educators Site where Everything is FREE!

- Facing Debt Collection? Know Your Rights

- Shining a Light on the Consumer Debt Industry

- World's Largest Debt Collector Pays the Price for Harassing Consumers

- A Little Credit

- You Owe Me Money

- FTC to Debt Collectors: Play by the Rules!

Consumer.gov articles (also available in Spanish):
- Managing Debt: What It Is; What To Know; What To Do

Just For You microsites:
- Consumer Advocates

- Financial Educators

Business Education

Blog Posts:
- When a data oops becomes an uh-oh

- Phantom of the owe-pera

- DONT VIOL8 FDCPA. K? THX

---

[32] Distribution statistics are not available for these materials.

Appendix B
Debt Collection Complaints Received Directly by the FTC[33]

Year	2013	2012
Total Debt Collection ("DC") Complaints	73,211	125,136
DC Complaints as Percentage of All FTC Complaints	17.0%	24.1%
Total Third-Party DC Complaints	60,485	102,783
Third-Party DC Complaints as Percentage of All FTC Complaints	14.0%	19.8%
Total In-House DC Complaints	12,726	22,353
In-House DC Complaints as Percentage of All FTC Complaints	2.9%	4.3%

---

[33] The Term "All FTC Complaints" refers to all industry-specific complaints received by the FTC in a given calendar year. It excludes identity theft and Do Not Call Registry complaints.

Appendix C
Debt Collection Complaints by FDCPA Complaint Category

FDCPA Complaint Category	Total 2013 Complaints	Percentage of 2013 FDCPA Complaints	2013 Category Rank	Total 2012 Complaints	Percentage of 2012 FDCPA Complaints	2012 Category Rank
Repeated Calls	23,582	39.0%	1	37,543	36.5%	2
Misrepresent Debt Character, Amount, or Status	23,068	38.1%	2	39,993	38.9%	1
Falsely Threatens Illegal or Unintended Act	20,627	34.1%	3	30,470	29.6%	3
No Written Notice	17,502	28.9%	4	26,139	25.4%	4
Falsely Threatens Arrest, Property Seizure	16,882	27.9%	5	24,062	23.4%	5
Fails to Identify as Debt Collector	11,941	19.7%	6	17,873	17.4%	6
Repeated Calls to Third Parties	10,026	16.6%	7	16,679	16.2%	7
Improperly Calls Debtor at Work	9,761	16.1%	8	14,482	14.1%	8
Uses Obscene, Profane, or Abusive Language	8,652	14.3%	9	13,329	13.0%	9
Reveals Debt to Third Party	8,571	14.2%	10	12,272	11.9%	10
Refuses to Verify Debt After Written Request	6,361	10.5%	11	9,814	9.5%	11
Collects Unauthorized Fees, Interest, or Expenses	5,605	9.3%	12	9,034	8.8%	12
Calls Before 8:00 a m., after 9:00 p m., or at Inconvenient Times	4,656	7.7%	13	8,166	7.9%	13
Calls Debtor After Getting "Cease Communication" Notice	2,906	4.8%	14	4,928	4.8%	14
Uses or Threatens Violence	2,502	4.1%	15	3,312	3.2%	15